Mastering

XRP

A Strategic Investor's Guide to Wealth, Risk and Analysis in Cryptocurrency

Unlocking Profits with XRP: Comprehensive Investment Strategies, RWA Management for Investors

Jon Erlaitz

ALSO BY JON ERLAITZ

XRP and the New Frontier of

Financial Inclusion

a Guide for Investors

an ebook for winners

Scan your gift at the end of this book with the QR

PUBLISHED BY: Power Finances 589

Under no circumstances will any blame or legal responsibility be held against the publisher, or author, for any damages, reparation, or monetary loss due to the information contained within this book. Either directly or indirectly. You are responsible for your own choices, actions, and results.

Legal Notice:

Disclaimer Notice:

Please note the information contained within this document is for educational and entertainment purposes only. All effort has been executed to present accurate, up to date, and reliable, complete information. No warranties of any kind are declared or implied. Readers acknowledge that the author is not engaging in the rendering of legal, financial, medical or professional advice. The content within this book has been derived from various sources.

Please consult a licensed professional before attempting any techniques outlined in this book.

By reading this document, the reader agrees that under no circumstances is the author responsible for any losses, direct or indirect, which are incurred as a result of the use of the information contained within this document, including, but not limited to, — errors, omissions, or inaccuracies.

The content of this book should not be considered investment advice. Investing is speculative. When investing, your capital is at risk.

To my Mother Ana,

Thank You for Promoting

The Best Values.

Jon Erlaitz

Content

Prologue

Hey there,

You know that feeling when you've been watching something incredible unfold right before your eyes, and the rest of the world is just starting to wake up? That's exactly where we are with XRP right now.

Look, we've all been through the crypto rollercoaster together. We've seen Bitcoin get all the headlines as "digital gold," watched Ethereum build its DeFi empire, and witnessed countless other projects come and go. But here's the thing that gets me excited every single day—XRP isn't just another crypto trying to find its place in the world. It's THE bridge that's actually connecting our old, clunky financial system to the lightning-fast, transparent future we all know is coming.

Think about it for a second. While everyone else was busy trying to replace traditional finance, Ripple and XRP took a completely different approach. They looked at the massive, trillion-dollar problem of moving money across borders—you know, those painful wire transfers that take forever and cost a fortune—and said, "What if we could make this instant, cheap, and transparent?"

And that's not just some pie-in-the-sky dream anymore. We're watching it happen in real time! Major banks, central banks, and payment providers are actually using XRP to solve real problems. Not just talking about it, not just running pilots—they're moving real money, right now, using our beloved digital asset.

What makes this even more incredible is that XRP isn't just about payments anymore. We're looking at a future where real-world assets—everything from real estate to commodities—can be tokenized and moved with the same speed and efficiency. Imagine unlocking liquidity in markets that have been stuck in the stone age for decades!

The XRP Army has been patient, we've weathered the storms, and we've kept the faith when others doubted. And you know what? That patience is about to pay off in ways that even the most optimistic among us might not have imagined.

This isn't just about making money (though let's be honest, that's pretty awesome too). This is about being part of something that's literally reshaping how the entire world thinks about value, money, and financial inclusion. When barriers between currencies start disappearing, when sending money becomes as easy as sending a text message, when people in developing countries can access the same financial tools as

Wall Street traders—that's when we'll know we backed the right horse.

Whether you've been hodling since the early days or you're just discovering what makes XRP special, you're about to dive into the story of how one digital asset is quietly revolutionizing the entire financial world. And trust me, this is just the beginning.

Welcome to the future, XRP Army. Our time is now!

X 1

1-Introduction to XRP

> *"We're building the Internet of value. Lock In."*
>
> ***— Brad Garlinghouse***

In today's rapidly evolving financial landscape, cryptocurrencies are no longer just speculative assets—they are becoming fundamental pil°lars in shaping the future of global finance. Among these digital currencies, **XRP** stands out as a key player, poised to revolutionize not only how money moves across borders but also how we interact with an emerging class of financial assets known as **Real World Assets (RWA)**.

The Evolving Financial Landscape

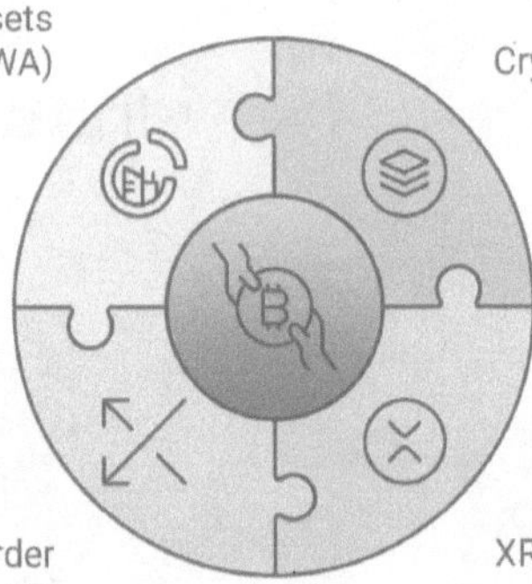

At its core, XRP was designed to facilitate instant, low-cost cross-border transactions, making it an essential tool for the global economy. Several financial institutions have already begun to integrate XRP into their payment systems, leveraging its ability to settle transactions in mere seconds compared to the days-long processes of traditional banking (Ripple, 2022). As this adoption continues, it is becoming increasingly clear that XRP is not just a speculative cryptocurrency, but a robust solution for the future of financial systems (Johnson, 2021).

However, perhaps even more exciting is how XRP is becoming intertwined with **Real World Assets (RWA)**. RWA refers to the process of digitizing physical, tangible assets—such as real estate, commodities, and equities—on blockchain platforms. This allows these assets to be tokenized and traded securely, unlocking liquidity and enabling a level of transparency and access that was previously unimaginable in traditional markets (Zhang et al., 2020).

The importance of RWAs lies in their potential to reshape financial markets by providing easier access and liquidity to previously illiquid or slow-moving assets. Tokenizing these assets can eliminate friction, enhance transparency, and lower costs associated with asset transfers and ownership (Sarkar & Desai, 2019). As we venture further into this era of tokenized finance, XRP's role in facilitating secure, scalable, and efficient transactions makes it a vital infrastructure layer for integrating these assets into the global financial ecosystem (Ahmed, 2021).

In this book, we will explore the multifaceted role XRP plays in the new financial paradigm, how RWAs are transforming investment strategies, and why these developments are crucial for investors seeking to thrive in a digital-first world. Whether you're an experienced investor or new to the realm of cryptocurrencies, understanding the combined impact of XRP and RWAs is key to navigating the future of finance.

References:

Ripple Whitepapers: Ripple frequently publishes whitepapers and reports on topics like XRP, tokenization, and the future of finance.

- Source: Ripple Insights

Academic Papers:

- Search academic databases like **Google Scholar**, **SSRN**, or **JSTOR** for peer-reviewed papers on XRP and blockchain tokenization.

Real World Asset (RWA) Tokenization Reports:

- The World Economic Forum (WEF) and Deloitte have reports on blockchain tokenization and RWAs.
- Source: WEF Tokenization Report

X 2

2-The History of XRP

Understanding Ripple's Journey from Start to Present

Cryptocurrencies have become a major part of today's digital economy, and XRP is one of the biggest names in the space. If you've heard about Bitcoin, you may have also come across XRP. While Bitcoin aims to replace traditional money, XRP has a different purpose, which we'll explain in this episode. Let's dive into the history of XRP, its founders, and some key moments in its development—explained in a way that anyone, even beginners, can understand.

What Is XRP and Why Was It Created?

XRP is the cryptocurrency associated with **Ripple Labs**, a technology company that focuses on making cross-border payments faster and cheaper. Unlike Bitcoin, which was created to give people a way to make digital payments without banks, XRP was made to **help banks** and **financial institutions** send money across the world more easily. Ripple's goal is to improve the current international banking system, making it more efficient.

Founders of XRP

Three developers, Arthur Britto, Jed McCaleb, and David Schwartz, started working on the XRP Ledger (XRPL) in 2011. Because they were intrigued by Bitcoin, they set out to improve upon its shortcomings in order to develop a more sustainable digital asset designed with payments in mind. And do not forget Chris Larsen that co-founded with McCaleb Opencoin the old name before Ripple. Here's a bit of background on them:

- **Chris Larsen**: A businessman with a history of working in financial technology. He became one of the richest people in the cryptocurrency world thanks to his involvement with Ripple.
- **Jed McCaleb**: A well-known figure in the crypto space, McCaleb also created the infamous Mt. Gox exchange (which later became a major Bitcoin exchange before it collapsed in

2014). He left Ripple in 2013 to start **Stellar**, another cryptocurrency project.

- **Arthur Britto**: Less public than Larsen and McCaleb, Britto is a cryptographer who helped build Ripple's technology.
- **David Schwartz**: is one of the key architects behind XRP and a prominent figure in the cryptocurrency space. Before co-founding **Ripple Labs**, Schwartz had a distinguished career in software engineering and cryptography. He worked as a software developer for **WebMaster Inc.**, where he built encrypted cloud storage systems, and later became a **Chief Technical Officer (CTO)** at Ripple Labs.

Key Dates in XRP's History

- **2011-2012: The Idea Behind Ripple**

Before XRP was even a thing, Jed McCaleb had the idea to create a faster, more efficient version of Bitcoin. He envisioned a network that wouldn't rely on energy-intensive mining (like Bitcoin) but would still use a form of cryptocurrency. This led to the creation of Ripple's technology.

- **2012: Ripple Is Born**

Ripple Labs was officially founded, and XRP was introduced as the network's cryptocurrency. The company aimed to create a system that could speed up international money transfers for banks, businesses, and payment services.

- **2013-2014: Early Growth**

Ripple began gaining attention in the financial world as an alternative to traditional banking systems like SWIFT (a global network that allows banks to send and receive information about financial transactions).

- **2014: Jed McCaleb's Departure**

Jed McCaleb left Ripple Labs due to disagreements with the rest of the team. He later founded **Stellar** (XLM), a cryptocurrency that shares some similarities with XRP.

- **2017: XRP's Price Boom**

The year 2017 saw a massive rise in cryptocurrency prices, and XRP was no exception. XRP reached an all-time high of nearly $3.84 in January 2018. This brought a lot of attention to Ripple, and people began seeing XRP as a potential competitor to Bitcoin and Ethereum.

- **2020: SEC Lawsuit Against Ripple**

In December 2020, the **U.S. Securities and Exchange Commission (SEC)** sued Ripple Labs, alleging that XRP was being sold as an unregistered security. This lawsuit caused a lot of uncertainty in the crypto market, and XRP's price dropped as several exchanges halted its trading. Ripple has been fighting the case ever since, and the final decision is still pending.

What Makes XRP Different?

To make it simple, here's how XRP stands out from other cryptocurrencies:

1. **Speed**: XRP transactions are extremely fast, taking only 3-5 seconds to process, while Bitcoin transactions can take up to 10 minutes or more.
2. **Cost**: It costs almost nothing to send XRP across the network, which is why banks are interested in using it for large, international transactions.
3. **No Mining**: Unlike Bitcoin, XRP doesn't need to be mined. All 100 billion XRP tokens were created at the start, and no more will ever be made. Bitcoin, on the other hand, has a mining process where new coins are generated.
4. **Target Market**: XRP was created to help **financial institutions** like banks, rather than focusing on everyday users. Its technology is aimed at improving the way money moves across borders, making it faster and cheaper.

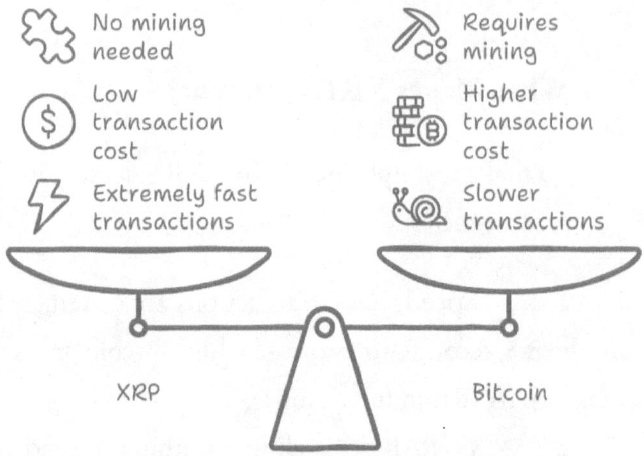

Key differences between XRP and Bitcoin.

Important Issues and Challenges XRP Has Faced

Like any other cryptocurrency, XRP hasn't had an easy journey. Here are some of the main challenges Ripple and XRP have faced:

1. **Centralization Concerns**:

One of the main criticisms of XRP is that it's more centralized than other cryptocurrencies. Ripple Labs holds a significant portion of XRP tokens, which gives it more control over the currency compared to Bitcoin, which is fully decentralized and controlled by no one.

2. **Legal Troubles with the SEC**:

The SEC's lawsuit is one of the biggest challenges Ripple has faced. The SEC claims that Ripple was selling XRP as an **unregistered security**, which means they believe it should be regulated like stocks or bonds. Ripple argues that XRP is a currency, not a security, and shouldn't be regulated this way. The outcome of this case could have a big impact on the future of XRP.

3. **Competition**:

Ripple isn't the only company trying to improve cross-border payments. Other cryptocurrencies like **Stellar (XLM)** and **SWIFT's new systems** are competitors. Ripple has to continuously improve its technology to stay ahead in the race.

4. **Volatility**:

Like all cryptocurrencies, the price of XRP is highly volatile. Its value can change rapidly, making it both an opportunity and a risk for investors.

Ripple's Partnerships and Global Reach

One of Ripple's biggest advantages is the number of partnerships it has with large financial institutions and banks worldwide. Ripple works with **over 300 financial institutions**, including well-known names like **Santander**, **American Express**, and **MoneyGram** (before MoneyGram paused its use of XRP due to the SEC lawsuit).

These partnerships highlight Ripple's ability to be used in real-world financial systems, which sets it apart from many other cryptocurrencies that are still trying to gain mainstream adoption.

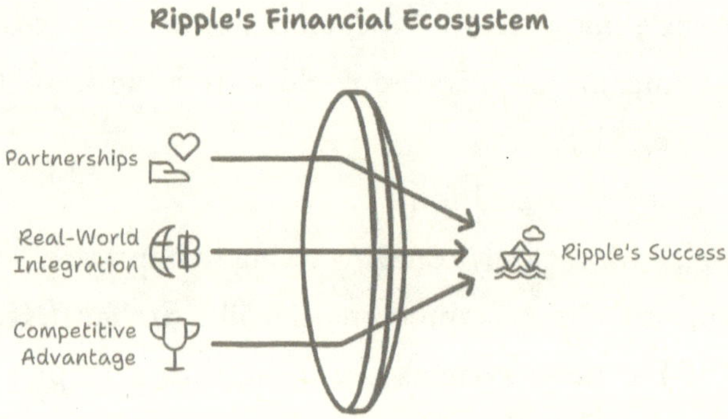

Why XRP Matters

In summary, XRP isn't just another cryptocurrency—it was created to solve a specific problem: improving the way money moves between banks and countries. While XRP and Ripple have faced their share of challenges, including legal issues and criticisms of centralization, they remain one of the biggest players in the crypto world. The future of XRP will largely depend on the outcome of the SEC lawsuit and Ripple's ability to maintain partnerships with financial institutions.

For beginners and those new to the crypto world, XRP offers a unique case study of how cryptocurrency can be used not just as a digital asset but also as a solution to real-world problems. Its journey from 2012 to today shows the potential, risks, and evolving nature of the crypto industry.

Jon Erlaitz

X 3

3-The Technology Behind XRP: How Ripple's Ledger Powers Fast and Efficient Transactions

In the world of cryptocurrency, the technology behind each coin is what sets them apart. XRP, developed by Ripple Labs, uses a unique system that allows it to process transactions quickly, efficiently, and with minimal cost. In this part, we will explore the technology behind XRP, explaining how it works and why it is considered one of the best solutions for cross-border payments. We'll also examine the **XRP Ledger Consensus Protocol** and how it compares to other methods like Bitcoin's Proof-of-Work. By the end, we'll see why this technology makes XRP a top contender for financial institutions worldwide.

XRP Ledger: What Makes It Different?

The foundation of XRP's speed and efficiency lies in its **XRP Ledger (XRPL)**, a decentralized, open-source blockchain technology designed for rapid transaction processing. Unlike other cryptocurrencies such as Bitcoin, which rely on energy-heavy mining to validate transactions, XRP uses a **consensus protocol** that does not require mining. This is a key factor in why XRP is able to settle transactions in a matter of seconds rather than minutes or hours.

Consensus Algorithm: The Core of XRP's Efficiency

What is a Consensus Algorithm?

A consensus algorithm is a process by which a network of computers (called nodes) agrees on the validity of transactions. In most cryptocurrencies, this is done through a Proof-of-Work (PoW) or Proof-of-Stake (PoS) system. Ripple, however, uses something different: the **XRP Ledger Consensus Protocol**.

How the XRP Consensus Algorithm Works

Unlike Bitcoin's Proof-of-Work, which requires miners to solve complex puzzles to validate transactions, XRP uses a system where independent validator nodes agree on which transactions are valid. These validators work together to reach a consensus on the state of the ledger (the record of transactions) approximately every 3 to 5 seconds.

Key points about XRP's consensus algorithm:

1. **No Mining**: Unlike Bitcoin, XRP does not need miners. This dramatically reduces the amount of energy required to maintain the network.
2. **Trusted Validators**: Ripple maintains a list of validators it trusts, but the network is decentralized, and anyone can run a validator. The consensus mechanism ensures that even if a few validators act maliciously, they cannot affect the integrity of the ledger.
3. **Low Latency**: The consensus protocol allows XRP transactions to be confirmed in mere seconds, making it one of the fastest cryptocurrencies for settlement times.
4. **Cost-Effective**: Because the network does not rely on resource-intensive mining, transaction fees are very low, often a fraction of a cent.

According to Ripple's documentation, the consensus process can handle **1,500 transactions per second (TPS)**, which is far superior to Bitcoin's average of **7 TPS** (Ripple, 2023). This makes XRP ideal for use cases like remittances and cross-border payments, where speed and low costs are essential (Ripple, 2023).

The Technology Stack of XRP Ledger

1. Nodes and Validators

The XRP Ledger operates with nodes that are responsible for validating transactions. Validator nodes, unlike in Bitcoin, don't compete with each other, and there's no mining process. Validators simply reach consensus based on the rules of the protocol, which keeps the network efficient.

2. XRP Ledger Objects and Transactions

The ledger itself is a decentralized database that contains all the transactions, balances, and accounts of users on the network. Every time a transaction is submitted, it gets added to the ledger, which is continuously updated as new transactions are confirmed.

3. Unique Node List (UNL)

Validators on the network use something called a **Unique Node List (UNL)** to agree on the current state of the ledger. The UNL is a list of trusted validators that each node believes to be reliable. This helps prevent fraud and attacks while ensuring transactions are processed quickly.

4. Interledger Protocol (ILP)

While not exclusive to XRP, Ripple supports the **Interledger Protocol (ILP)**, which is designed to connect different ledgers and payment systems globally. ILP acts as a bridge between various payment networks, allowing XRP to be used for transactions that involve different currencies. It enhances Ripple's mission of streamlining cross-border transactions by providing a universal standard.

Why XRP's Technology Is Ideal for Transactions

1. Fast Settlement Times

XRP transactions are processed within 3-5 seconds, which is crucial in financial environments where time equals money. Traditional cross-border payment systems like SWIFT can take several days to settle a payment, but XRP's consensus protocol allows for near-instant settlements. According to Ripple's technical papers, this makes XRP one of the fastest cryptocurrencies available today (Ripple, 2022).

2. Low Transaction Fees

Another significant advantage of XRP is its **minimal transaction costs**. Each transaction on the XRP Ledger costs a tiny fraction of an XRP (often less than $0.001). This is a big selling point for financial institutions looking to reduce the overhead costs associated with sending money internationally. This is in stark contrast to Bitcoin, where transaction fees can spike during periods of high network demand (Ripple, 2021).

3. Scalability

The XRP Ledger can handle 1,500 transactions per second, which makes it one of the most scalable blockchains in existence today. This means XRP is not only fast and cheap but also capable of processing high volumes of transactions without slowing down. For comparison, Visa, one of the world's largest payment networks, handles around 1,700 transactions per second, so XRP is on par with traditional systems (Ripple, 2022).

WRA: XRP's Role in the Wider Ripple Ecosystem

The **WRA (XRP Ledger Consensus)** protocol, combined with Ripple's suite of technologies like **RippleNet**, allows XRP to serve as a bridge currency in cross-border transactions. This means it can facilitate payments between different currencies by converting them into XRP, speeding up the settlement process and reducing the costs involved.

Ripple's use of XRP as part of its **On-Demand Liquidity (ODL)** service is a prime example of how the WRA system functions in practice. ODL allows banks and financial institutions to move money instantly across borders without the need to hold pre-funded accounts in foreign currencies, using XRP as a bridge between different fiat currencies (Ripple, 2023).

Why XRP's Technology Stands Out for Cross-Border Payments

1. Energy Efficiency

Unlike Bitcoin's energy-intensive Proof-of-Work, XRP's consensus protocol is extremely energy-efficient. Since there is no need for mining, XRP can process transactions without consuming vast amounts of electricity. This makes XRP more sustainable and eco-friendly, which is becoming an increasingly important consideration for financial institutions (Ripple, 2021).

2. Security and Reliability

XRP's consensus mechanism ensures that transactions are validated securely. While Ripple does control some aspects of the validator network through the Unique Node List (UNL), the system is still decentralized enough to prevent any single entity from taking control. This balance between decentralization and efficiency allows XRP to offer fast, reliable transactions while maintaining a secure ledger (Ripple, 2020).

3. Wide Adoption

XRP's technology has already gained traction among banks and financial institutions worldwide. More than **300 financial institutions** are partnered with Ripple to use its technology for faster cross-border payments, demonstrating the real-world utility and effectiveness of the XRP Ledger (Ripple, 2021).

Why XRP's Technology Is Superior for Transactions

XRP's underlying technology, particularly its **XRP Ledger Consensus Protocol**, sets it apart from other cryptocurrencies when it comes to cross-border transactions. Its speed, scalability, and cost-efficiency make it one of the best solutions for financial institutions looking to modernize their payment systems. By eliminating the need for energy-hungry mining, XRP is both eco-friendly and fast, offering near-instant settlement times with minimal transaction costs. Additionally, with its ability to act as a bridge currency through On-Demand Liquidity, XRP proves itself as a powerful tool for cross-border payments, streamlining international money transfers while reducing costs.

For these reasons, XRP's technology is seen as a game-changer in the world of finance, providing a blockchain solution that works seamlessly within existing financial systems while also offering a more sustainable and efficient approach to global transactions.

X 4

4-The Advantages of XRP Over Other Cryptocurrencies

As the cryptocurrency space continues to evolve, various digital currencies serve different purposes, and their underlying technology can significantly impact their performance and efficiency. XRP, the digital asset developed by Ripple Labs, is widely known for its fast and low-cost transactions, especially in cross-border payments. This episode explores the **advantages of XRP** over other major cryptocurrencies like Bitcoin, Ethereum, Solana, and others, analyzing transaction performance, efficiency, and failures. By understanding where XRP excels, we can see why it has become a go-to solution for financial institutions and global payments.

1. Transaction Speed: XRP vs. Other Cryptocurrencies

XRP's Speed

One of XRP's standout features is its **transaction speed**. With the ability to settle transactions in **3-5 seconds**, XRP is among the fastest cryptocurrencies. This speed is due to its **XRP Ledger Consensus Protocol**, which reaches an agreement on the validity of transactions without needing the slow, energy-intensive mining process used by Bitcoin and Ethereum.

Bitcoin's Speed

By contrast, **Bitcoin** suffers from much slower transaction speeds. Bitcoin's **Proof-of-Work (PoW)** consensus mechanism requires miners to solve complex mathematical puzzles to validate transactions. As a result, Bitcoin can only process **about 7 transactions per second (TPS)**, with confirmation times that can take anywhere from **10 minutes to an hour** or more, especially when the network is congested. In periods of high traffic, this can be even longer.

Ethereum's Speed

Ethereum, despite being faster than Bitcoin, still faces **scalability issues**. In its current form (before Ethereum 2.0's full rollout), Ethereum processes **about 30 TPS**, with confirmation times ranging from **15 seconds to 5 minutes**. However, network congestion during times of high demand can lead to much longer wait times and skyrocketing fees, a major issue that users experience during periods of increased traffic, such as during NFT drops or DeFi spikes.

Solana's Speed

Solana is another high-performance blockchain that boasts **a staggering 65,000 TPS** under ideal conditions. Solana uses a **Proof-of-History (PoH)** consensus combined with **Proof-of-Stake (PoS)** to achieve such high throughput. However, while Solana excels in terms of transaction speed, its network has experienced performance issues, as discussed below.

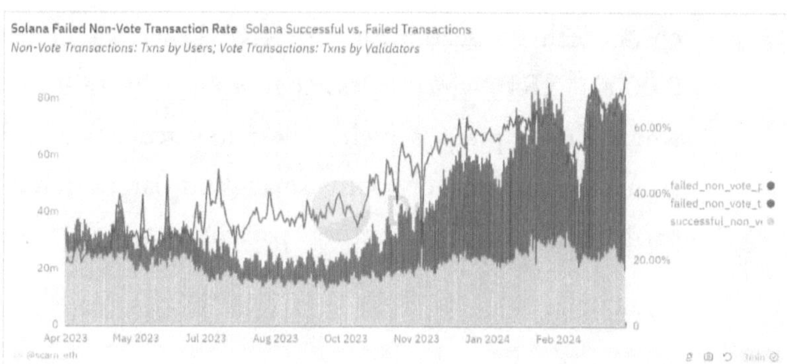

Solana non-vote transactions fail rate from Apr 2023 to May 2024.

Source: @scarn_eth & Dune Analytics

XRP Advantage: Real-Time Transaction Settlement

XRP's ability to process **1,500 TPS** with **3-5 second settlement times** places it well ahead of Bitcoin and Ethereum and competitive with Solana. For financial institutions that require fast settlements for cross-border payments, XRP provides a real-time, scalable solution that balances both speed and reliability.

2. Transaction Fees: Low Costs of XRP vs. Expensive Gas Fees

XRP's Low Fees

Another area where XRP shines is in its **low transaction costs**. Each transaction on the XRP Ledger incurs a fee of **0.00001 XRP**, which is **less than a fraction of a cent** even when XRP's price is high. These low fees make XRP an attractive option for both small and large transactions, particularly for cross-border payments where traditional systems like SWIFT often have high fees and slow settlement times.

Bitcoin's High Fees

Bitcoin's transaction fees vary depending on network congestion and can range from a few dollars to over **$20 per transaction** during periods of high demand. These fees are a result of the limited block size (1 MB) and the competition among miners to include transactions in the next block. As more users compete for block space, fees increase, making Bitcoin impractical for small or frequent transactions.

Ethereum's Gas Fees

Ethereum faces even higher fees, often referred to as **gas fees**. During periods of high network activity, Ethereum gas fees can soar into the hundreds of dollars for a single transaction. This makes Ethereum prohibitively expensive for most users during high-demand periods, as seen during the 2021 DeFi boom and NFT craze.

Solana's Fees

Solana offers relatively low transaction fees compared to Ethereum and Bitcoin, with average fees of **$0.00025 per transaction**. However, Solana's low fees come with occasional network reliability issues, as we'll discuss in the next section.

XRP Advantage: Consistent, Minimal Fees

XRP's ability to maintain **minimal, predictable fees** gives it a significant advantage over Bitcoin and Ethereum, especially for users looking to avoid the unpredictability of gas fees. XRP's fees remain nearly zero even during periods of high usage, making it a cost-effective solution for global financial transactions.

3. Transaction Failures and Network Downtime: Stability of XRP vs. Other Networks

XRP's Stability

One of XRP's greatest strengths is the **stability and reliability** of the XRP Ledger. Because the network does not rely on mining and uses a more energy-efficient consensus protocol, the risk of delays or failures is minimal. The XRP Ledger rarely experiences network downtime or performance issues, which is crucial for institutions that need a reliable means of transferring large sums of money across borders.

Bitcoin's Transaction Failures

Bitcoin is relatively stable in terms of network uptime, but during periods of congestion, transactions can experience delays or **fail entirely** if users do not pay high enough fees. Transactions that sit in the **mempool** (a waiting area for unconfirmed transactions) for too long may be dropped altogether. While Bitcoin's security is robust, its slow and inefficient transaction process makes it less than ideal for high-speed payments.

Ethereum's Network Congestion

Ethereum has also been plagued by **network congestion** and **transaction failures** during peak times. When gas fees spike, many users' transactions fail to get processed unless they pay higher fees to prioritize their transaction. This issue makes Ethereum unreliable for real-time transactions when the network is under heavy load.

Solana's Downtime Issues

Despite its high-speed performance, **Solana** has experienced **multiple network outages** since its launch, with some lasting several hours. These outages are often due to bugs or congestion overwhelming the network. For example, in September 2021, the network was down for **over 17 hours**, leading to concerns about Solana's long-term reliability.

XRP Advantage: Consistent Performance with Minimal Downtime

XRP has a strong track record of maintaining consistent performance, with few reports of downtime or transaction failures. This makes XRP one of the most reliable cryptocurrencies for fast and frequent transactions, particularly in the cross-border payments sector. Unlike Solana's downtime issues or Ethereum's high failure rates during congestion, XRP is dependable for institutions that cannot afford delays or failures.

4. Environmental Efficiency: XRP's Sustainability vs. Proof-of-Work Cryptos

XRP's Energy Efficiency

XRP's consensus algorithm is not only faster but also **far more energy-efficient** than Bitcoin's Proof-of-Work. Since

XRP does not rely on mining, it consumes minimal electricity, making it one of the more **eco-friendly cryptocurrencies**. This is increasingly important as environmental concerns around Bitcoin's energy consumption continue to grow.

Bitcoin's High Energy Consumption

Bitcoin's Proof-of-Work system is notoriously energy-hungry. According to some estimates, Bitcoin consumes as much energy as the entire country of Argentina (University of Cambridge, 2021). This raises serious environmental concerns and has led some companies to stop accepting Bitcoin due to its environmental impact.

Ethereum's Move to Proof-of-Stake

Ethereum is in the process of transitioning to **Ethereum 2.0**, which will replace its current Proof-of-Work system with a more energy-efficient **Proof-of-Stake (PoS)** model. This should significantly reduce Ethereum's energy consumption, but the transition is not yet complete, and Ethereum's current model remains energy-intensive.

Solana's Energy Profile

Solana's **Proof-of-History (PoH)** combined with Proof-of-Stake (PoS) consumes significantly less energy than Bitcoin and Ethereum. However, it still requires energy to validate transactions, although much less than traditional Proof-of-Work systems.

XRP Advantage: Sustainable, Low-Energy Consensus

XRP's minimal energy consumption is a key advantage over Bitcoin and Ethereum, making it a more sustainable choice for those concerned with the environmental impact of blockchain technology. With no need for mining, XRP offers an eco-friendly alternative without compromising on speed or security.

Conclusion: Why XRP Outperforms Other Cryptocurrencies in Transactions

In conclusion, **XRP's** transaction performance and efficiency give it several clear advantages over Bitcoin, Ethereum, Solana, and other major cryptocurrencies. With **fast settlement times, low transaction fees**, and a **reliable, energy-efficient network**, XRP is uniquely suited to handle cross-border payments and financial transactions on a global scale.

- **Bitcoin** is often seen as a store of value but struggles with slow transaction speeds and high fees, making it less practical for daily use.

- **Ethereum** offers more flexibility with smart contracts but faces crippling gas fees and congestion during high usage periods.
- **Solana** boasts impressive speed and low fees but suffers from occasional network downtime, raising questions about its long-term reliability.

For users and institutions seeking a reliable, fast, and cost-effective way to transfer money globally, **XRP stands out** as one of the most efficient and scalable solutions in the cryptocurrency world. Its technology offers a **sustainable** and **real-world utility** that few other cryptocurrencies can match.

Jon Erlaitz

X 5

5-The Role of XRP in the Future of Finance

Revolutionizing Global Bank Transactions

In the rapidly evolving world of finance, blockchain technology is increasingly being recognized as a game-changer, especially in the realm of bank transactions. Among the various digital currencies available, **XRP** stands out for its ability to transform cross-border payments and create a more efficient financial system. Paired with the upcoming **ISO 20022** standard, XRP holds the potential to replace outdated systems like **SWIFT**, setting the stage for faster, more cost-effective, and secure global transactions.

In this part, we'll explore how XRP is playing a key role in shaping the future of finance, the significance of ISO 20022, and how the SWIFT system may soon be replaced by these advancements.

The Current State of Global Bank Transactions: SWIFT's Limitations

For decades, the **SWIFT (Society for Worldwide Interbank Financial Telecommunication)** system has been the backbone of global banking transactions, connecting over 11,000 financial institutions in more than 200 countries. SWIFT essentially serves as the messaging network that facilitates cross-border payments between banks. It doesn't actually move the money itself but ensures that the message about the payment reaches the correct institution.

While SWIFT has been a reliable system for years, it is increasingly viewed as outdated for several reasons:

1. **Slow Processing Times**: SWIFT transactions can take anywhere from **1 to 5 business days** to complete, depending on the banks involved, the countries, and the currency being transferred.
2. **High Fees**: SWIFT payments often involve multiple intermediaries (correspondent banks), each charging their own fees. This can make international transactions expensive, especially for smaller payments.
3. **Lack of Transparency**: Once a payment is initiated through SWIFT, it can be difficult to track its status

until the transaction is completed. This lack of transparency can lead to uncertainty for both banks and customers.

4. **Complexity**: SWIFT uses a variety of message formats, making it harder for financial institutions to maintain consistent communication, and increasing the risk of errors or delays.

In the face of these challenges, the banking world is looking for alternatives, and that's where **XRP** and **ISO 20022** come into play.

XRP: A Game Changer for Cross-Border Payments

XRP, the cryptocurrency developed by **Ripple Labs**, is specifically designed to solve the inefficiencies of cross-border payments. Its blockchain, known as the **XRP Ledger**, allows financial institutions to transfer value across borders quickly and at a fraction of the cost compared to traditional systems like SWIFT.

Key Benefits of XRP for Global Bank Transactions

1. **Speed**: XRP transactions are settled in **3-5 seconds**, which is a massive improvement over SWIFT's 1-5 day settlement times. This speed is a critical advantage for financial institutions that need to move money internationally in real-time.

2. **Low Costs**: Unlike SWIFT, which often involves multiple intermediaries each charging fees, XRP transactions have **minimal transaction costs** (fractions of a cent). This makes XRP a highly cost-effective solution for both small and large-scale transactions.

3. **Transparency**: The XRP Ledger provides full transparency and real-time tracking of payments, enabling banks to know the exact status of a transaction at any given time. This is something SWIFT has been criticized for lacking.

4. **On-Demand Liquidity (ODL)**: Ripple's **On-Demand Liquidity (ODL)** service allows financial institutions to leverage XRP as a bridge currency, eliminating the need for **pre-funded nostro and vostro accounts**. This frees up capital and simplifies the cross-border transaction process by converting money into XRP and then into the destination currency almost instantly.

References:

According to Ripple, their ODL service has already been adopted by over **300 financial institutions**, and the use of XRP in cross-border payments has resulted in significantly reduced costs and transaction times for these banks (Ripple, 2023).

ISO 20022: The New Global Financial Standard

The importance of **ISO 20022** cannot be overstated in the context of modernizing financial messaging and transactions. ISO 20022 is a **global messaging standard** for financial transactions, set to replace many existing standards used by institutions like SWIFT. It enables a more **structured and data-rich format** for financial messages, making payments more transparent, automated, and efficient.

Key Features of ISO 20022:

1. **Data-Rich Messaging**: Unlike previous messaging formats, ISO 20022 allows for **richer data content** in financial messages. This means that each transaction can carry more detailed information, improving the accuracy of payments and reducing the likelihood of errors.
2. **Global Standardization**: ISO 20022 is designed to be a **global standard**, meaning that all participating financial institutions will use the same messaging format. This is crucial for simplifying international payments, as it ensures consistency across borders and reduces the need for multiple formats.
3. **Automation**: The improved data structure in ISO 20022 allows for more **automated processing** of payments, cutting down on manual intervention and reducing the risk of

human error. This will streamline bank operations and improve the efficiency of global transactions.

4. **Interoperability**: ISO 20022 is highly **interoperable** with different payment systems, allowing it to integrate with both traditional financial institutions and new players in the space, like Ripple. This compatibility makes it ideal for the future of global finance.

How XRP and ISO 20022 Work Together

XRP and **ISO 20022** are a powerful combination for revolutionizing the global banking system. As banks adopt ISO 20022 to standardize their messaging protocols, XRP can act as the digital asset that powers real-time, cross-border transactions. Ripple, the company behind XRP, has positioned itself to align with the ISO 20022 standards, ensuring that its solutions are compatible with the future of global payments.

Ripple's Role in ISO 20022

Ripple has made sure that its technology aligns with the ISO 20022 standard, making it one of the few blockchain companies to be part of the **ISO 20022 standards body** (Ripple, 2023). This means that Ripple's solutions, including those using XRP, are designed to be compatible with the new messaging formats that banks around the world will soon be required to adopt.

With this alignment, financial institutions can use **RippleNet**, Ripple's global payment network, to handle cross-border transactions in a way that meets the requirements of ISO 20022, offering a more **seamless, automated**, and **transparent** process than traditional systems.

The Future of SWIFT: Will It Be Replaced?

With the rise of **blockchain technology** and the adoption of **ISO 20022**, many are wondering whether **SWIFT** will continue to dominate the world of international bank payments. While SWIFT has been slow to adapt, it is far from being replaced overnight. However, the introduction of technologies like **XRP** poses a serious challenge to SWIFT's dominance.

SWIFT's Adoption of ISO 20022

SWIFT has acknowledged the need to modernize and has begun rolling out **ISO 20022** to its network. This move will allow SWIFT to stay relevant in the face of competition from blockchain technologies. However, SWIFT's underlying framework still relies on traditional correspondent banking relationships, meaning that it can't compete with the speed and efficiency of blockchain solutions like XRP.

SWIFT vs. XRP: A Head-to-Head Comparison

Feature	SWIFT	XRP
Transaction Speed	1-5 business days	3-5 seconds
Transaction Fees	High fees due to intermediaries	Minimal fees (fractions of a cent)
Transparency	Low, difficult to track	Real-time transaction tracking
Efficiency	Complex, requires multiple banks	Simple, on-demand liquidity
Alignment with ISO 20022	In transition to ISO 20022	Already aligned with ISO 20022

As this table shows, XRP has several advantages over SWIFT, particularly in speed, cost, and transparency. While SWIFT may continue to modernize, its reliance on old systems makes it difficult to compete with blockchain technologies in the long run.

Conclusion: XRP and ISO 20022—Paving the Way for the Future of Finance

XRP and ISO 20022 are at the forefront of a financial revolution. As banks begin adopting the ISO 20022 messaging standard, the need for faster, more efficient payment systems will grow. **XRP**, with its ability to settle transactions in real-time and at minimal cost, provides a **solution that SWIFT cannot currently match**.

By combining **XRP's blockchain technology** with the global standardization of **ISO 20022**, Ripple is poised to become a key player in the future of international bank payments. For financial institutions looking to improve their cross-border transaction systems, XRP represents a faster, cheaper, and more reliable alternative to SWIFT. The future of finance will be driven by technologies like XRP, which not only align with global standards but also push the boundaries of what's possible in banking.

In the coming years, as more banks transition to ISO 20022 and explore blockchain solutions, **XRP may well**

emerge as the foundation of the next-generation financial system, offering a level of efficiency and speed that was previously unattainable.

X 6

6-The Legal Landscape of XRP

Global Perspectives with a Focus on the USA, UK, and BRICS Nations

Understanding XRP's Regulatory Challenges and Opportunities Across the World

The rise of cryptocurrencies has brought not only technological innovations but also legal challenges, especially as governments grapple with how to regulate digital assets like **XRP**. XRP, created by **Ripple Labs**, has garnered significant attention due to its potential to transform cross-border payments. However, its global legal status remains in flux. In this part, we will explore the legal landscape surrounding XRP, with a particular focus on the **United States**, the **United Kingdom**, and the **BRICS** nations (Brazil, Russia, India, China, and South Africa). Understanding the regulatory frameworks in these regions is crucial to XRP's future in the global financial system.

XRP's Legal Framework: A Global Overview

As XRP's popularity has grown, regulators across the globe have taken varied approaches to its classification and regulation. XRP's use case as a **bridge currency** in cross-border payments makes it unique, but this also places it in a regulatory gray area. Globally, the legal treatment of XRP largely falls into two categories: whether it is classified as a **currency**, **commodity**, or a **security**.

- **Currency**: Some nations view XRP as a digital currency used for facilitating payments, much like how traditional fiat currencies operate.
- **Commodity**: In a few countries, XRP is treated as a commodity, regulated similarly to gold or oil.
- **Security**: In others, notably the United States, there are ongoing debates as to whether XRP should be classified as a security, which would subject it to much stricter regulations.

Each of these classifications has significant implications for XRP's use, trading, and adoption. Below, we'll take a closer look at how different jurisdictions, particularly the **USA**, **UK**, and **BRICS nations**, are approaching XRP from a legal standpoint.

The United States: XRP and the SEC Lawsuit

In the United States, XRP's legal standing is defined by its battle with the **Securities and Exchange Commission (SEC)**. This legal case is not only crucial for XRP but for the entire cryptocurrency industry, as it could set a precedent for how digital assets are regulated in the U.S.

The SEC Lawsuit: Background

In **December 2020**, the SEC filed a lawsuit against **Ripple Labs**, alleging that XRP was being sold as an **unregistered security**. The SEC's argument hinges on the **Howey Test**, a legal principle used to determine whether an asset qualifies as a security. The SEC contends that Ripple's sale of XRP constitutes an **investment contract**, and therefore, XRP should be regulated as a security, much like stocks or bonds.

Ripple, on the other hand, argues that XRP is a **digital currency**, akin to Bitcoin or Ethereum, both of which the SEC has classified as commodities, not securities. Ripple further claims that the SEC's lawsuit has caused market confusion and harm to XRP holders, as many exchanges delisted the token due to the uncertainty.

The Impact of the Lawsuit

The SEC lawsuit has significantly impacted XRP's market in the U.S.:

•**Delisting**: Major exchanges such as **Coinbase** and **Binance.US** temporarily delisted XRP, limiting its availability to U.S. investors.

•**Market Volatility**: The legal uncertainty has caused price swings, as investors weigh the potential outcomes of the case.

•**Ripple's Defense**: Ripple Labs has mounted a robust defense, arguing that XRP is a utility token used for facilitating payments, not an investment contract. Ripple has gained support from the **XRP community** and filed documents showing that the SEC's previous actions suggested ambiguity over how digital assets should be treated.

Potential Outcomes

There are several potential outcomes of the lawsuit:

1. **SEC Victory**: If the SEC wins, XRP would likely be classified as a security, and Ripple would face significant fines. XRP's use in the U.S. could be restricted, and exchanges would be required to register XRP as a security before trading it.

2. **Ripple Victory**: If Ripple wins, it would set a positive precedent for XRP and other cryptocurrencies in the U.S., potentially leading to increased adoption and investment in the sector.

3. **Settlement**: A settlement between the SEC and Ripple could result in a more favorable regulatory framework for XRP, avoiding the need for a court ruling but imposing certain restrictions on Ripple's operations.

United Kingdom: A More Favorable Regulatory Climate

In contrast to the U.S., the **United Kingdom** has taken a more progressive approach to regulating digital assets, including XRP. The UK's regulatory stance is shaped by its efforts to establish itself as a global leader in fintech and blockchain innovation.

XRP as an Exchange Token

In the UK, XRP is classified as an **exchange token** by the **Financial Conduct Authority (FCA)**. Exchange tokens are not considered securities and are used primarily for payments and trading. This classification provides XRP with more regulatory clarity in the UK compared to the U.S. XRP is not subject to the same stringent regulations as securities, making it easier for exchanges and financial institutions to use and trade it.

The UK's Approach to Digital Asset Regulation

The FCA has been relatively hands-off when it comes to regulating exchange tokens like XRP, though it has taken measures to protect consumers from fraudulent schemes and ensure financial stability:

- **Consumer Protections**: The FCA has issued warnings about the risks of investing in cryptocurrencies, but it has not imposed heavy restrictions on their use or trading.
- **Sandbox Initiatives**: The FCA has established a **regulatory sandbox** that allows fintech companies, including those involved with blockchain and digital assets, to test their products in a controlled environment. Ripple has participated in these initiatives, further solidifying its presence in the UK financial market.

Overall, the UK provides a **business-friendly environment** for XRP and other cryptocurrencies, allowing for innovation while maintaining some degree of oversight.

BRICS Nations: Diverse Approaches to XRP and Cryptocurrency Regulation

The **BRICS nations** (Brazil, Russia, India, China, and South Africa) represent some of the world's largest emerging economies. Each country has its own approach to cryptocurrency regulation, reflecting different political, economic, and technological priorities. Let's examine the legal landscape for XRP in these countries:

Brazil: A Growing Market for XRP

Brazil is one of the most crypto-friendly countries in the BRICS bloc. The Brazilian government has taken steps to regulate cryptocurrencies while promoting innovation in the fintech space:

- **Regulatory Clarity**: Brazil does not consider cryptocurrencies like XRP to be legal tender but has provided a regulatory framework that treats them as **digital assets**. This has allowed exchanges and financial institutions to adopt cryptocurrencies for various use cases, including cross-border payments.
- **Ripple Partnerships**: Ripple has forged partnerships with Brazilian banks and financial institutions to leverage XRP for cross-border transactions, capitalizing on the country's open regulatory environment.

Russia: Tightening Regulations Amid Sanctions

Russia has had a complicated relationship with cryptocurrencies, including XRP. While Russia has not outright banned cryptocurrencies, the regulatory environment is becoming increasingly restrictive:

• **Ban on Crypto Payments**: In 2020, Russia passed a law banning the use of cryptocurrencies as a method of payment. However, they are still allowed for trading and investment purposes.

• **Government Control**: Russian authorities have expressed interest in launching a **digital ruble**, potentially reducing the role of decentralized cryptocurrencies like XRP in the country. The government's desire to maintain control over financial systems has limited XRP's use in the country.

India: Legal Uncertainty but Growing Adoption

India has historically been uncertain about how to regulate cryptocurrencies, including XRP. However, recent developments suggest that the government may be shifting towards more lenient regulations:

• **Previous Bans**: India's central bank had previously banned banks from dealing with cryptocurrencies, but this ban was overturned by the **Supreme Court** in 2020.

- **New Regulations Expected**: India is currently drafting new legislation to regulate cryptocurrencies, with proposals ranging from outright bans to more comprehensive regulation. Ripple has expressed interest in the Indian market, particularly in providing solutions for remittances and cross-border payments.
- **Potential for Growth**: With one of the largest populations in the world and a significant remittance market, India could be a key player for XRP if favorable regulations are implemented.

China: The Strictest Stance in BRICS

China has taken one of the most stringent approaches to cryptocurrency regulation, banning almost all crypto-related activities:

- **Ban on Mining and Trading**: China banned cryptocurrency mining in 2021 and has severely restricted the trading of digital assets, including XRP.
- **Centralized Digital Yuan**: Instead of cryptocurrencies, China is focusing on its own **central bank digital currency (CBDC)**, the **digital yuan**, which is intended to replace traditional cryptocurrencies for domestic payments.

China's tight control over financial activities leaves little room for decentralized cryptocurrencies like XRP to operate, making it one of the least favorable markets for Ripple.

South Africa: A Balanced Approach

South Africa has taken a balanced approach to cryptocurrency regulation, providing a framework for the use and trading of digital assets like XRP:

- **Regulatory Clarity**: South Africa's **Financial Sector Conduct Authority (FSCA)** has issued guidance on how cryptocurrencies should be treated, emphasizing the need for consumer protection while allowing for innovation.
- **Crypto Adoption**: South Africa has seen a rise in the adoption of cryptocurrencies, including XRP, for cross-border payments and investment purposes. The government has also signaled interest in regulating the sector to encourage more institutional participation.

XRP's Legal Future in a Fragmented Global Landscape

The legal landscape for XRP remains complex and fragmented, with significant differences between countries and regions. In the **United States**, the outcome of the **SEC lawsuit** will have a profound impact on XRP's future, potentially setting a legal precedent for how other digital assets are treated. Meanwhile, the **United Kingdom** offers a more favorable regulatory environment, classifying XRP as an **exchange token** with fewer restrictions. The **BRICS nations** present a mixed bag, with some countries, like **Brazil**, welcoming XRP, while others, like **China**, have implemented heavy restrictions.

As global financial systems evolve, the regulatory clarity around digital assets like XRP will play a crucial role in determining their adoption and use in banking and cross-border payments. Despite the current legal challenges, XRP has the potential to revolutionize the way money moves across borders, but it will need to navigate a complex web of global regulations to fully realize this potential.

X 7

7-The SEC vs. XRP: A Legal Battle

The world of cryptocurrencies has seen its fair share of regulatory hurdles, but few cases have attracted as much attention as the ongoing legal battle between the **Securities and Exchange Commission (SEC)** and **Ripple Labs**, the company behind the cryptocurrency **XRP**. The outcome of this lawsuit could set a precedent for how digital assets are regulated in the United States and may have profound implications for the entire cryptocurrency industry.

In this section, we will break down the origins of the lawsuit, the arguments from both sides, and the potential consequences for XRP, Ripple, and the broader crypto market.

What Is the SEC vs. Ripple Lawsuit About?

The lawsuit dates back to **December 2020**, when the **SEC** filed a complaint against **Ripple Labs**, its CEO **Brad Garlinghouse**, and co-founder **Chris Larsen**. The SEC alleges that Ripple had been selling **XRP** as an **unregistered security** since its creation, and that these sales amount to illegal securities offerings worth **$1.3 billion**.

The SEC's core argument is based on the **Howey Test**, a legal principle used to determine whether a financial asset qualifies as an "investment contract" and, therefore, a security. The Howey Test requires that an asset meet four criteria to be considered a security:

1. **Investment of money**
2. **In a common enterprise**
3. **With the expectation of profit**
4. **From the efforts of others**

The SEC claims that XRP fits these criteria, arguing that Ripple's continuous sales of XRP are a securities offering, and thus Ripple should have registered XRP with the commission.

Ripple's Response

Ripple has strongly denied these allegations, arguing that XRP is not a security but rather a **digital currency** like **Bitcoin (BTC)** or **Ethereum (ETH)**. Ripple maintains that XRP functions as a bridge currency for facilitating cross-border payments and that it operates independently of Ripple's control. Ripple asserts that XRP is a **utility token** used for real-world purposes, not an investment vehicle.

Ripple's defense centers around several key points:

1. **XRP is similar to Bitcoin and Ethereum**, both of which the SEC has publicly stated are **not securities**.
2. **The sale of XRP** does not constitute an investment contract, as holders of XRP do not have ownership in Ripple or expect profits solely from Ripple's actions.
3. **The SEC's inconsistent stance**: Ripple has pointed out that the SEC did not issue clear regulatory guidance on XRP for several years, which created uncertainty in the market.

Key Developments in the SEC vs. Ripple Lawsuit

1. Ripple's Fair Notice Defense

A major component of Ripple's legal strategy is its **Fair Notice Defense**, which argues that the SEC failed to provide adequate notice that XRP would be considered a security under U.S. law. Ripple claims that the lack of clarity surrounding the SEC's rules on digital assets misled the company and investors into believing that XRP was a compliant cryptocurrency.

Ripple has bolstered its argument by referencing public statements made by the SEC about **Bitcoin** and **Ethereum**, both of which the SEC determined to be commodities, not securities. Ripple contends that XRP is fundamentally similar to these cryptocurrencies, further challenging the SEC's rationale for treating it differently.

2. Hinman's Speech and Internal Documents

One of the most controversial aspects of the case revolves around a speech given in **2018** by the SEC's former director of corporate finance, **William Hinman**. In his speech, Hinman declared that **Ethereum** was no longer considered a security because it had become sufficiently decentralized.

Ripple's legal team has requested access to **internal SEC communications** related to this speech, hoping to prove that the SEC's decision-making process about XRP has been inconsistent and arbitrary.

In a key ruling, the court allowed Ripple access to these internal documents, which could provide Ripple with evidence to support its Fair Notice Defense. If these documents reveal that the SEC was unclear about XRP's status, it could significantly weaken the SEC's case.

3. Impact on the Market

Following the SEC's lawsuit, several major cryptocurrency exchanges, including **Coinbase**, **Binance.US**, and **Kraken**, suspended or delisted XRP trading in the United States. The legal uncertainty caused XRP's price to plummet, though it has since recovered much of its value as Ripple continues to fight the case.

Despite the ongoing legal challenges, Ripple's **cross-border payment solution** using XRP, known as **On-Demand Liquidity (ODL)**, continues to expand globally, with partnerships in regions like **Asia**, **Europe**, and **Latin America**.

Potential Outcomes of the SEC vs. Ripple Case

The SEC vs. Ripple case could end in several different ways, each of which would have a significant impact on the future of XRP and the broader cryptocurrency industry.

1. SEC Wins

If the SEC wins, XRP would be classified as a security. This would have serious consequences for Ripple and XRP holders:

- Ripple would likely face significant **financial penalties** for selling unregistered securities.
- XRP would be subject to **securities regulations** in the U.S., making it more difficult to trade on cryptocurrency exchanges. Many U.S.-based exchanges could continue to delist XRP, reducing its liquidity and adoption.
- Ripple would likely be required to **register XRP with the SEC**, a process that could take time and further complicate its use as a bridge currency for international payments.

2. Ripple Wins

If Ripple prevails in the lawsuit, XRP could continue to operate as a digital currency, not a security. This would be a major victory for Ripple and the cryptocurrency industry:

• XRP could be **relisted on major exchanges** in the U.S., leading to increased liquidity and a likely rise in price.

• A Ripple victory could set a **precedent** for how other cryptocurrencies are regulated, potentially leading to more favorable conditions for digital assets across the U.S. market.

• Ripple's **On-Demand Liquidity (ODL)** platform would likely continue to grow, with financial institutions more willing to adopt XRP for cross-border payments.

3. Settlement

A **settlement** between the SEC and Ripple is another possible outcome. In this scenario:

• Ripple might agree to pay a fine without admitting any wrongdoing, allowing XRP to continue trading as a digital asset.

• The SEC may issue **clearer guidelines** on how XRP and other cryptocurrencies are classified in the future.

• This outcome could provide **regulatory clarity** for XRP without a definitive court ruling, though it may leave unresolved questions about the status of other cryptocurrencies.

Implications for the Cryptocurrency Industry

The outcome of the SEC vs. Ripple case will not only affect XRP but could also have **far-reaching consequences** for the entire cryptocurrency industry in the United States. If the SEC succeeds in classifying XRP as a security, other cryptocurrencies may come under similar scrutiny, forcing companies to **register** their tokens as securities and adhere to stringent regulatory requirements.

On the other hand, if Ripple wins, it could lead to **greater clarity and leniency** in how digital assets are regulated, potentially encouraging more innovation and adoption in the U.S. cryptocurrency market.

A Legal Battle to Shape the Future

The SEC vs. Ripple lawsuit represents one of the most important legal battles in the history of cryptocurrency. Its outcome will likely determine how digital assets are regulated in the United States, with implications for XRP holders, Ripple's business, and the broader crypto landscape.

As the case progresses, investors, exchanges, and legal experts will be watching closely to see whether XRP will emerge from this legal storm as a regulatory pioneer or a cautionary tale. Regardless of the final verdict, the lawsuit underscores the need for clearer regulations and greater legal certainty in the rapidly evolving world of cryptocurrency.

Key Points Summary: The SEC vs. XRP Legal Battle

- **Lawsuit Overview**:
  - The **SEC filed a lawsuit against Ripple Labs** in December 2020, claiming that **XRP is an unregistered security**.
  - The SEC argues Ripple sold $1.3 billion worth of XRP as an investment contract, violating U.S. securities laws.
- **Ripple's Defense**:
  - Ripple asserts that **XRP is a digital currency**, similar to **Bitcoin** and **Ethereum**, not a security.
  - Ripple claims **XRP has utility as a bridge currency** for cross-border payments and is not tied to investment profits.
  - **Fair Notice Defense**: Ripple argues the SEC did not provide clear guidance on XRP, leading to market confusion.
- **Key Developments**:
  - Ripple was granted access to **internal SEC documents**, particularly related to a 2018 speech where **Ethereum** was declared not a security.
  - Major U.S. cryptocurrency exchanges, like **Coinbase** and **Binance.US**, suspended XRP trading after the lawsuit.

- **Potential Outcomes**:
  - **SEC Wins**: XRP is classified as a security, Ripple faces fines, and XRP would need to comply with strict securities regulations.
  - **Ripple Wins**: XRP remains a **digital currency**, relisted on exchanges, and Ripple's business could expand, setting a precedent for other cryptocurrencies.
  - **Settlement**: Ripple could pay fines but continue operating, with no definitive court ruling on XRP's status.
- **Broader Implications**:
  - The case could set a **legal precedent for the regulation of cryptocurrencies** in the U.S.
  - A win for Ripple might provide **regulatory clarity** for other digital assets, while an SEC win could lead to **stricter regulations** across the crypto industry.
- **Ripple's Ongoing Business**:
  - Despite the lawsuit, Ripple's **On-Demand Liquidity (ODL)** platform continues to grow globally, especially in regions outside the U.S.

X 8

8-The Ripple Effect: How XRP Impacts Other Cryptocurrencies

XRP has been in the news lately because of a legal dispute it has with the Securities and Exchange Commission (SEC) of the United States. Even if the case's decision is still up in the air, it will have a big impact on the worldwide financial scene as well as the larger bitcoin industry. But what's going on with other cryptocurrencies and XRP?

The growing global acceptance of the ISO 20022 standard by financial organizations is one important consideration. This standard aims to simplify and enhance cross-border payments by offering a common language for financial operations. Wide-ranging effects might result from its deployment, such as the possibility of upending established financial institutions and creating new chances for cryptocurrencies.

How ISO 20022 Impacts XRP and the Crypto Market

- **Improved Interoperability:** The implementation of ISO 20022 has the potential to greatly improve interoperability between various payment systems and financial institutions. This may promote cross-border transfers more easily, which might be advantageous for cryptocurrencies like XRP that want to enable quick and affordable international payments.
- **Enhanced Competition:** Traditional banks may see an increase in their level of competition in the cross-border payments sector when they implement ISO 20022. Lower costs and quicker transaction times might result from this, placing pressure for cryptocurrencies to provide value propositions that are on par with or better than them.

•**Regulatory Difficulties:** Cryptocurrency regulations may face obstacles from the introduction of ISO 20022. Regulators may find it harder to control and monitor cross-border cryptocurrency transactions as traditional financial institutions becoming more integrated. This can result in more stringent rules or limitations on particular cryptocurrencies.

The Ripple Effect

There will probably be a variety of effects of ISO 20022 on XRP and the larger cryptocurrency industry. Cross-border payments may be significantly impacted by XRP if it can effectively negotiate its legal issues and take advantage of its possible advantages. But there will also be a lot of obstacles to overcome because to the growing rivalry from conventional banks and the changing regulatory environment.

Implementation of ISO 20022

The adoption of ISO 20022 is a game changer in the global financial environment. It has significant ramifications for cryptocurrencies such as XRP. Being able to provide distinctive value propositions will be crucial for cryptocurrencies as traditional banks became more competitive in the cross-border payments market. The result of the SEC lawsuit against XRP and the state of the regulatory landscape at large will be very important in deciding how this coin and the cryptocurrency ecosystem as a whole develop.

The cryptocurrency space is a dynamic ecosystem where different digital assets interact, influence, and compete with each other. Among the prominent players is **XRP**, the digital token created by Ripple Labs, which has carved a unique niche in the world of blockchain through its focus on **cross-border payments** and **financial institutions**. XRP's speed, scalability, and low transaction fees make it a central player in reshaping global finance. However, its influence extends beyond its own ecosystem, impacting other major cryptocurrencies and blockchain projects.

This article explores **how XRP impacts various cryptocurrencies**, including **Bitcoin (BTC), Ethereum (ETH), Tether (USDT)**, and others. Additionally, we'll take a closer look at XRP's role in shaping projects like **World Real Assets (WRA)**, which aims to bridge the gap between **blockchain technology** and **real-world assets**.

XRP's Influence on Major Cryptocurrencies

XRP and Bitcoin (BTC)

Bitcoin is widely recognized as the **store of value** in the cryptocurrency world, often referred to as "digital gold." While Bitcoin's main utility is as a long-term asset, XRP's core use case lies in **instantaneous payments** and **liquidity provision**. XRP's ability to settle transactions within **seconds** compared to Bitcoin's average **10-minute block confirmation time** has challenged Bitcoin's position as the preferred method for transferring large sums internationally. However, instead of replacing Bitcoin, XRP has found a complementary role, serving as a **bridge currency** in transactions involving BTC, particularly when used for cross-border remittances.

XRP and Ethereum (ETH)

While **Ethereum** is known for its **smart contracts** and decentralized applications (dApps), XRP's focus on **speed** and **low fees** for financial transfers offers an attractive alternative for certain applications, particularly in traditional finance. XRP's consensus algorithm, which doesn't require mining, allows for **greater scalability**, often seen as a challenge for Ethereum, especially during high-traffic periods. However, Ethereum's transition to **Ethereum 2.0** could bring significant improvements in speed and scalability, potentially altering the dynamic between the two.

XRP and Stablecoins (USDT, USDC)

XRP also impacts **stablecoins** like **Tether (USDT)** and **USD Coin (USDC)**, which are pegged to the US dollar and are used extensively in the crypto market for trading and hedging. XRP's role as a **bridge currency** in the **RippleNet** network enables faster and cheaper transactions involving stablecoins. In fact, many institutions that rely on Ripple's payment solutions use XRP to facilitate **settlements** between different fiat currencies, thereby boosting **liquidity** for stablecoins in the global market.

XRP's Impact on Emerging Cryptocurrencies

XRP and Solana (SOL)

Solana is known for its **high transaction throughput** and low fees, positioning itself as a competitor in the world of **decentralized finance (DeFi)** and non-fungible tokens (NFTs). While Solana's speed is remarkable, XRP's **institutional partnerships** and regulatory compliance provide it with a different competitive edge. XRP's enterprise-grade solutions and its ability to facilitate **cross-border payments** at scale could potentially influence

Solana's growth, especially as traditional financial institutions explore blockchain options.

XRP and Cardano (ADA)

Cardano, with its emphasis on **academic research** and a **proof-of-stake** consensus model, represents a more decentralized approach compared to XRP. However, XRP's established presence in the banking and financial services sectors could influence how Cardano positions itself in the market. Ripple's success in securing **global partnerships** with banks and financial institutions could create pressure on projects like Cardano to align their development efforts with real-world applications, especially in sectors like finance and governance.

XRP and Dogecoin (DOGE)

Dogecoin gained notoriety due to its status as a meme coin and its **community-driven** growth. While Dogecoin lacks the serious institutional use cases of XRP, it still benefits from Ripple's broader push to **normalize cryptocurrency** as a payment method. Ripple's strides in improving crypto adoption in payment solutions indirectly lend legitimacy to coins like Dogecoin, which have been experimenting with **merchant adoption** for small-scale transactions.

XRP's Influence on World Real Assets (WRA)

The **World Real Assets (WRA)** project represents a groundbreaking attempt to **tokenize real-world assets** and bring them into the blockchain ecosystem. XRP's impact on projects like WRA can be understood through its role in **facilitating fast, cost-effective, and scalable transactions**. Let's break down some key areas of influence:

XRP as a Bridge Currency for Real Assets

RippleNet and XRP serve as a powerful **payment network** for financial institutions, and this can extend into the world of **real-world asset tokenization**. WRA's aim to tokenize assets such as **real estate, commodities, and physical infrastructure** can benefit from XRP's liquidity solutions. By using XRP as a **bridge currency**, WRA can efficiently facilitate the **transfer of value** between various asset classes and national currencies, ensuring **seamless cross-border payments**.

Enabling Global Liquidity

One of the biggest challenges for tokenizing real assets is ensuring adequate **liquidity**. XRP's ability to serve as an **intermediary currency** allows for the **instant conversion** of one fiat or cryptocurrency into another. This could be particularly valuable for WRA, where buyers and sellers may come from **different regions** or may want to transact in **multiple currencies**. Ripple's focus on **regulatory compliance** also makes XRP an attractive option for WRA's institutional clients, ensuring that real-world assets can be bought and sold with **transparency and security**.

Smart Contracts and Asset Management

Although XRP is not primarily a **smart contract platform**, its ability to integrate with **decentralized oracles** and platforms like **Chainlink (LINK)** enables XRP to support **asset management solutions** for tokenized assets. Projects like WRA can benefit from XRP's **transaction efficiency** while leveraging other blockchain technologies for the execution of **smart contracts** that govern the ownership and transfer of real assets.

The Ripple Effect on Other Projects and Cryptocurrencies

XRP's influence is not limited to established players like **Bitcoin** and **Ethereum** or emerging projects like **WRA**. Here's a brief look at how XRP influences other notable cryptocurrencies:

• **Polygon (MATIC)**: XRP's fast cross-border payments may complement Polygon's **layer-2 scaling solutions**, making global transfers on Ethereum more efficient.

• **Polkadot (DOT)**: XRP's cross-chain functionality could enhance Polkadot's focus on **interoperability**, helping assets move across different blockchains.

• **Avalanche (AVAX)**: XRP's **enterprise-focused use case** challenges Avalanche's position as a fast DeFi platform, particularly in the realm of large institutional transfers.

• **Litecoin (LTC)**: XRP's focus on institutional adoption has the potential to overshadow Litecoin's niche as a **fast payment coin**.

• **Chainlink (LINK)**: XRP could benefit from Chainlink's **oracle services**, further enhancing its position in **real-world data integration** for enterprise solutions.

XRP's influence in the cryptocurrency space extends far beyond its role as a payment token. As a bridge currency for **cross-border payments** and a key player in **institutional finance**, XRP has the potential to **reshape the competitive landscape** of the crypto world. Its impact on major cryptocurrencies like Bitcoin and Ethereum highlights its role in **enhancing transaction efficiency**, while its influence on emerging projects like **World Real Assets (WRA)** underscores its potential to bring **real-world asset tokenization** to life.

As the crypto market continues to evolve, XRP's ongoing **development** and its ability to foster **global liquidity** will likely increase its prominence, leaving a lasting ripple effect across the entire cryptocurrency ecosystem.

X 9

9-The XRP Community: Who Are They and What Do They Believe?

The XRP community is one of the most passionate and dedicated groups within the cryptocurrency space. This community has grown exponentially since the inception of Ripple Labs and the creation of XRP, with individuals from various backgrounds coming together to support, advocate, and promote what they believe to be a revolutionary financial technology. But who makes up the XRP community, and what exactly do they believe in?

The Origins of the XRP Community

The origins of the XRP community can be traced back to the early days of Ripple Labs, founded in 2012. Early adopters of XRP saw its potential to transform the way cross-border payments were conducted. As Ripple's mission to create faster, more efficient payment solutions gained traction, the

XRP community began to take shape, growing steadily with the launch of RippleNet and its On-Demand Liquidity (ODL) service. Over time, the community has evolved into a global movement that shares a strong belief in XRP's utility for real-world financial applications.

Who Makes Up the XRP Community?

The XRP community is diverse and consists of several key groups. First, there are investors and traders who believe in XRP's long-term value, driven by its utility in financial ecosystems. These individuals often actively participate in social media forums and engage in discussions about the price movements and market trends surrounding XRP. Developers and technologists also play a significant role in the community, focusing on the technical potential of XRP and contributing to its development on the XRP Ledger. Financial institutions and corporations that partner with Ripple, such as banks and payment processors, represent another facet of the community, recognizing the advantages of XRP for cross-border transactions. Finally, social media influencers, advocates, and everyday users form the backbone of the XRP Army, a group that vigorously supports the token through various online channels, spreading information and rallying behind the project.

Key Figures and Influencers in the XRP Community

Prominent figures within the XRP community include both independent influencers and key executives at Ripple. On social media platforms like Twitter, several influential accounts have emerged, driving discussions and debates around XRP. These influencers help educate the broader public about XRP's technology, potential, and challenges. Meanwhile, Ripple's leadership, particularly CEO Brad Garlinghouse and CTO David Schwartz, are viewed as champions of the project. Their regular communication and updates on Ripple's progress keep the community engaged and hopeful for the future.

The XRP Community's Core Beliefs

At the heart of the XRP community's beliefs is the conviction that XRP is the future of cross-border payments. Unlike many other cryptocurrencies that are primarily seen as speculative investments, XRP is valued for its real-world utility. The community strongly believes that XRP's speed, low transaction costs, and scalability make it ideal for global financial transactions. Additionally, they emphasize the idea that XRP has a unique role as a bridge currency, helping to facilitate seamless transfers between different fiat currencies and cryptocurrencies.

Despite Ripple's significant influence over XRP's ecosystem, the community maintains a delicate balance between embracing the company's contributions and advocating for the decentralization of the XRP Ledger. Many in the community view Ripple as a necessary partner that has fostered institutional adoption, but they are also vocal about the importance of maintaining a decentralized network where users can participate independently of Ripple's actions.

Ripple and the XRP Community's Relationship

The relationship between Ripple, the company, and the XRP community is both supportive and complex. While Ripple's efforts to promote XRP's use in cross-border payments have earned the community's admiration, some members remain cautious about the company's level of control over XRP. This duality has sparked debates about decentralization within the community. Many XRP supporters, however, see Ripple's corporate partnerships with major banks and financial institutions as crucial steps toward legitimizing and expanding the use of XRP on a global scale.

Ripple vs. SEC: Community Reactions and Beliefs

One of the most defining moments in the history of the XRP community was the SEC's lawsuit against Ripple in late 2020, accusing the company of selling XRP as an unregistered security. This lawsuit triggered a widespread reaction within the community, with many rallying behind Ripple, claiming that the case was unfair and harmful to innovation in the crypto space. The XRP Army, in particular, became vocal advocates for regulatory clarity, calling for the relisting of XRP on several exchanges that had delisted the token amid the legal uncertainty. The community remains optimistic about the outcome of the case, with many believing that a favorable ruling could lead to a surge in adoption and price.

The Utility of XRP According to the Community

The XRP community firmly believes in the token's utility beyond its role as a speculative asset. For them, XRP is a means to achieve faster, cheaper, and more secure cross-border payments, especially for financial institutions. Ripple's On-Demand Liquidity (ODL) service, which leverages XRP as a bridge currency, is frequently cited by the community as a game-changer for global finance. The community envisions a future where XRP is widely used not only by banks but also by payment processors and other entities looking to streamline international transactions. They argue that XRP's unique characteristics make it superior to many other digital assets, particularly for use cases requiring liquidity and speed.

The XRP Community and Real-World Assets (RWAs)

Another aspect of the XRP community's belief system revolves around the tokenization of real-world assets (RWAs) on the blockchain. Many in the community view XRP as a key player in the movement to bring traditional financial assets, such as real estate, commodities, and even fiat currencies, onto the blockchain. They see this as a way to unlock liquidity and create more efficient markets, with XRP serving as a bridge for these assets in a decentralized financial system. The potential for XRP to facilitate the transfer and exchange of RWAs is a major point of optimism among community members.

XRP in DeFi: A Community Perspective

The rise of decentralized finance (DeFi) has prompted many XRP enthusiasts to consider how the token could integrate into the rapidly growing DeFi ecosystem. While XRP is not yet as widely used in DeFi as Ethereum or other tokens, the community is excited about its potential in this space. They believe that XRP's scalability and speed make it a prime candidate for DeFi applications, such as lending, staking, and decentralized exchanges. Additionally, some in the community are hopeful that future developments on the

XRP Ledger could bring smart contract functionality, further expanding XRP's role in DeFi.

XRP vs. Other Cryptocurrencies: A Community Debate

Within the XRP community, there is a strong belief that XRP is uniquely positioned to outperform other cryptocurrencies, especially in the realm of payments. Many community members contrast XRP with Bitcoin and Ethereum, pointing out XRP's lower transaction fees, faster settlement times, and energy efficiency. They argue that while Bitcoin and Ethereum have their own merits, XRP's design makes it the most practical choice for real-world financial use cases. This comparison fuels debates within the community about the future of cryptocurrencies and the distinct advantages that XRP holds over its competitors.

Social Media and the XRP Community

Social media platforms play a crucial role in uniting and mobilizing the XRP community. Twitter, in particular, is home to a vibrant network of XRP supporters who use hashtags like #XRPArmy, #RelistXRP, and #XRPCommunity to spread awareness and engage in discussions. Reddit, YouTube, and Telegram are also popular channels where the community shares news, analyses, and opinions about XRP's developments. Memes and trends play a significant role in the XRP community's online presence, helping to foster a sense of camaraderie and shared mission among its members.

Key Movements and Campaigns within the XRP Community

One of the most notable movements within the XRP community has been the #RelistXRP campaign, which emerged in response to the SEC lawsuit and the subsequent delisting of XRP from several cryptocurrency exchanges. The campaign was aimed at encouraging exchanges to relist XRP, arguing that the lawsuit had unfairly stigmatized the token. Beyond this, the community has also been active in promoting regulatory clarity and pushing for broader adoption of XRP in financial systems around the world. Many members see themselves as advocates for financial inclusion, with XRP playing a role in democratizing access to banking services.

XRP Community's Vision for the Future

Looking to the future, the XRP community envisions a world where XRP is the backbone of global finance, seamlessly facilitating cross-border payments and asset transfers. They believe that as regulatory clarity improves and more institutions adopt Ripple's technology, XRP will play an increasingly important role in the global economy. The community is optimistic about the token's long-term prospects, predicting widespread adoption in both traditional finance and the emerging decentralized finance space.

Criticisms and Challenges Facing the XRP Community

Despite the enthusiasm, the XRP community faces its fair share of challenges and criticisms. Chief among these is the perception of centralization, with critics pointing to Ripple's large holdings of XRP and its influence over the network. Additionally, the volatility of XRP's price and the ongoing legal uncertainty surrounding the SEC lawsuit have been persistent hurdles for the community. However, supporters remain undeterred, arguing that these challenges are temporary and that XRP's long-term value will be realized through its utility and adoption.

The Community's Broader Impact on the Crypto Space

The influence of the XRP community extends beyond just supporting one token. Through their advocacy, education efforts, and social media presence, they have helped shape broader discussions about cryptocurrency regulation, real-world asset tokenization, and the future of digital payments. The community's emphasis on utility over speculation has also contributed to shifting the narrative around the value of cryptocurrencies in the real world. As the crypto space continues to evolve, the XRP community is likely to remain a significant force in shaping the future of finance.

The XRP community is a vibrant and dedicated group that believes in the transformative potential of XRP. Whether through promoting its use in cross-border payments, advocating for regulatory clarity, or exploring new use cases in decentralized finance and real-world asset tokenization, the community remains united in its vision for a future where XRP plays a pivotal role in the global financial system. While they face challenges, their unwavering support and belief in XRP's utility will likely continue to drive its adoption and evolution in the years to come.

X 10

10-The Risks of Investing in XRP

The world of cryptocurrencies presents both incredible opportunities and substantial risks. Among the myriad of options available, **XRP**, the native digital currency of the **Ripple network**, is one of the most talked-about assets in the crypto market. While XRP has its unique value proposition, especially its focus on revolutionizing cross-border payments, it is not immune to the volatility and risks inherent in the cryptocurrency market.

This article delves deep into the specific risks associated with investing in XRP, helping potential investors understand the challenges they may face and make more informed decisions.

1. Regulatory Uncertainty: The Ripple vs. SEC Lawsuit

One of the most significant risks facing XRP investors is the ongoing **legal battle between Ripple Labs and the U.S. Securities and Exchange Commission (SEC)**. This lawsuit, filed in December 2020, alleges that Ripple conducted an unregistered securities offering by selling XRP. If the courts rule that XRP is a security, Ripple Labs could face massive fines, and XRP's legal status in the U.S. could be severely impacted.

Why This Matters to Investors:

- If XRP is classified as a security, it could face tighter regulations, making it more difficult to trade and potentially limiting its market access.
- Exchanges might delist XRP or restrict its trading to avoid legal ramifications, which could negatively affect liquidity and price.

This legal uncertainty creates significant market risk. While Ripple has scored some legal victories, the case is ongoing, and the outcome could have long-term repercussions for the token.

2. Market Volatility: Price Swings and Speculation

Like most cryptocurrencies, XRP is subject to extreme price volatility. It is not uncommon to see massive price swings in a single day, driven by speculation, news, or broader market sentiment.

Factors Contributing to XRP's Volatility:

- **News and Rumors**: Positive or negative news about Ripple's legal issues or partnerships can trigger significant price movements.
- **Market Sentiment**: As a top-10 cryptocurrency by market cap, XRP is heavily influenced by the overall sentiment in the cryptocurrency market. Bullish or bearish movements in Bitcoin or Ethereum often ripple through to affect XRP's price.
- **Low Liquidity in Some Markets**: In certain regions or exchanges, the liquidity of XRP can be relatively low, amplifying price fluctuations.

For investors, this volatility means that their investments can gain or lose significant value in a short time, posing risks for those without a high-risk tolerance.

3. Dependence on Ripple Labs

XRP's future is closely tied to the success and actions of **Ripple Labs**, the company behind the cryptocurrency. Ripple's main focus is developing solutions for **cross-border payments** using XRP. However, this heavy reliance on Ripple as a company creates centralized risk, unlike Bitcoin, which operates on a decentralized network without a single point of failure.

Potential Risks:

- **Company Performance**: If Ripple Labs faces financial issues, regulatory challenges, or strategic failures, XRP could suffer.
- **Concentration of Holdings**: A large portion of XRP is held by Ripple Labs and its executives. This concentration gives them substantial control over the supply, raising concerns about centralization and market manipulation.

Ripple's role in promoting and developing the XRP ecosystem is both a strength and a potential vulnerability. If Ripple Labs were to collapse or face restrictions, XRP's value could plummet.

4. Competitive Landscape in Cross-Border Payments

Ripple's core use case for XRP is to enable **faster and cheaper cross-border transactions**. However, the company is not the only player in this space. Traditional financial systems like **SWIFT** and new blockchain competitors like **Stellar (XLM)** are also vying for dominance in the cross-border payment market.

Challenges in the Space:

- **Incumbent Institutions**: Major financial institutions are often slow to adopt new technologies like blockchain. While Ripple has made some partnerships, broader industry adoption of XRP for cross-border payments remains limited.
- **Emerging Competitors**: Other blockchain projects are offering similar services. Stellar, for instance, has a similar goal but operates on a decentralized platform, potentially making it more attractive to some users.

If Ripple cannot continue to secure high-profile partnerships or drive the adoption of XRP in real-world use cases, it could lose its competitive edge, making the asset less valuable in the long term.

5. Centralization Concerns

Although XRP is often marketed as a decentralized cryptocurrency, critics argue that **Ripple Labs exercises too much control** over the currency. The large XRP holdings by Ripple executives and the company itself contribute to these concerns. Additionally, Ripple's consensus mechanism, while efficient for its intended use cases, is seen as less decentralized than Bitcoin's proof-of-work or Ethereum's proof-of-stake mechanisms.

Why Decentralization Matters:

- **Security**: Decentralized networks are generally considered more secure because they are less prone to manipulation or attack.
- **Censorship Resistance**: True decentralization ensures that no single entity can control the network, freeze assets, or censor transactions.

For investors seeking cryptocurrencies that fully embody decentralization principles, XRP's reliance on Ripple Labs may be a red flag.

6. Exchange Delistings and Liquidity Risks

The regulatory uncertainty surrounding XRP has already led to **some exchanges delisting the token**, particularly in the U.S. market. Major platforms like **Coinbase** suspended trading of XRP following the SEC lawsuit, leading to concerns about liquidity for investors.

Consequences of Delisting:

- **Reduced Market Access**: Fewer exchanges offering XRP means reduced trading options for investors.
- **Liquidity Risks**: Lower trading volume and limited exchange listings can make it more difficult to buy or sell XRP without impacting the price.
- **Global Impact**: Even though the lawsuit is centered in the U.S., global exchanges may follow suit if the regulatory situation worsens.

For investors, the possibility of future delistings, especially on major platforms, poses a significant liquidity risk.

7. Technological Risks and Network Attacks

While Ripple's technology is generally seen as robust, no blockchain network is immune to technical risks or attacks. **Network security** is a critical concern, and while Ripple uses a consensus mechanism known as **Ripple Protocol Consensus Algorithm (RPCA)**, it is still susceptible to certain types of attacks.

Potential Technological Risks:

- **Bugs or Vulnerabilities**: Like any software, Ripple's code could contain bugs or vulnerabilities that malicious actors might exploit.
- **Network Downtime**: In the unlikely event of a network outage, XRP transactions could be delayed or halted, affecting investors' ability to move their funds.

Technological risks, while less prominent than regulatory and market risks, remain a concern for any cryptocurrency investment, including XRP.

8. The Uncertain Future of Cryptocurrency Regulation

Beyond the SEC lawsuit, the broader regulatory environment for cryptocurrencies remains highly uncertain. Governments around the world are developing new policies to regulate crypto assets, and XRP, as one of the largest cryptocurrencies by market cap, is likely to be affected by these regulations.

Potential Regulatory Risks:

- **Tighter Government Control**: Future regulations could impose stricter compliance requirements on XRP exchanges, wallets, and transactions.
- **Tax Implications**: Changing tax laws could affect how XRP is treated, potentially leading to higher tax liabilities for investors.

For investors, the evolving regulatory landscape introduces an additional layer of risk, making it more challenging to predict XRP's future.

9. Long-Term Viability Concerns

Finally, one of the most fundamental questions facing XRP is its long-term viability. While Ripple has developed a unique and potentially valuable technology for cross-border payments, the long-term success of XRP as a cryptocurrency remains uncertain.

Key Questions:

- **Will XRP be widely adopted for real-world use?**
- **Can Ripple continue to navigate its legal and competitive challenges?**

•Will regulatory authorities classify XRP as a security, and how will this impact its market?

For long-term investors, these questions are critical when assessing the potential risks and rewards of holding XRP.

FAQs About Investing in XRP

1. Is XRP a good long-term investment?

•XRP has potential, but its long-term value depends on legal outcomes, market adoption, and competition. Investors should consider the high risks involved.

2. Can XRP be delisted from more exchanges?

•Yes, especially if the SEC lawsuit results in XRP being classified as a security, more exchanges could delist the token.

3. What happens if XRP is classified as a security?

•If XRP is classified as a security, Ripple may face fines, and trading restrictions could be imposed, limiting liquidity and price growth. But according to the

4. How does XRP differ from Bitcoin?

•XRP is faster and more efficient for cross-border payments but faces centralization concerns, unlike Bitcoin, which is fully decentralized.

5. Is Ripple's lawsuit with the SEC still ongoing?

•As of now, the case is ongoing, and the outcome remains uncertain. Investors should stay informed about developments.

6. What makes XRP more volatile than other cryptocurrencies?

•XRP's price volatility is influenced by its legal issues, market sentiment, and the actions of Ripple Labs, leading to sharper price swings than some other cryptocurrencies.

Jon Erlaitz

X 11

11-XRP Vs BTC: Which One is Better?

Navigating the Distinct Worlds of Ripple and Bitcoin to Determine the Superior Cryptocurrency

In the ever-evolving landscape of cryptocurrencies, Bitcoin (BTC) and Ripple's XRP stand out as two of the most prominent and widely discussed digital assets. While both aim to revolutionize the way we perceive and use money, they cater to different needs and operate on distinct principles. This article delves into the key differences, strengths, and weaknesses of XRP and BTC to help you determine which cryptocurrency aligns better with your investment goals and usage preferences.

1. Origin and Purpose

Bitcoin (BTC)

●Created By: An anonymous entity known as Satoshi Nakamoto in 2009.

●Purpose: Designed as a decentralized digital currency to facilitate peer-to-peer transactions without the need for intermediaries like banks. Bitcoin aims to be "digital gold," serving as a store of value.

XRP (Ripple)

●Created By: Ripple Labs Inc., co-founded by Chris Larsen and Jed McCaleb in 2012.

●Purpose: Developed to enable fast, low-cost international money transfers between financial institutions. XRP acts as a bridge currency to facilitate liquidity in cross-border transactions.

2. Technology and Scalability

Bitcoin (BTC)

●Blockchain: Utilizes a Proof-of-Work (PoW) consensus mechanism, which requires significant computational power.

- Transaction Speed: Processes approximately 5-7 transactions per second (TPS).
- Scalability: Limited scalability has led to higher transaction fees and slower processing times during peak demand.

XRP (Ripple)

- Ledger Technology: Employs the Ripple Protocol Consensus Algorithm (RPCA), which is more energy-efficient compared to PoW.
- Transaction Speed: Capable of handling 1,500 TPS with transaction settlements in mere seconds.
- Scalability: Highly scalable, making it suitable for large-scale financial operations and cross-border payments.

3. Decentralization

Bitcoin (BTC)

- Decentralization: Highly decentralized with thousands of nodes across the globe ensuring network security and integrity.
- Control: No single entity controls Bitcoin, aligning with its ethos of decentralization and censorship resistance.

XRP (Ripple)

- Decentralization: More centralized compared to Bitcoin, as Ripple Labs holds a significant portion of XRP tokens and has substantial influence over the network.
- Control: Ripple Labs plays a pivotal role in the development and direction of the XRP ecosystem, which has raised concerns about centralization among some critics.

4. Use Cases

Bitcoin (BTC)

- Primary Use: Investment and store of value; often referred to as "digital gold."
- Secondary Uses: Peer-to-peer transactions, remittances, and as a hedge against economic instability in some regions.

XRP (Ripple)

- Primary Use: Facilitating cross-border payments and liquidity management for financial institutions.

• Secondary Uses: Microtransactions, micropayments, and as a bridge currency in decentralized finance (DeFi) applications.

5. Market Performance and Adoption

Bitcoin (BTC)

• Market Dominance: Bitcoin remains the largest cryptocurrency by market capitalization.

• Adoption: Widely accepted by various merchants, institutional investors, and even some governments. Seen as the gateway cryptocurrency for many new investors.

XRP (Ripple)

• Market Position: Among the top cryptocurrencies by market cap, though it has faced legal challenges that have impacted its adoption.

• Adoption: Used primarily by banks and financial institutions for efficient cross-border transactions. However, ongoing legal battles with the SEC have affected its market perception and adoption.

6. Legal and Regulatory Challenges

Bitcoin (BTC)

- Regulatory Status: Generally recognized and accepted in many jurisdictions, though regulatory stances can vary.
- Challenges: Faces scrutiny over potential use in illicit activities and concerns about environmental impact due to PoW mining.

XRP (Ripple)

- Regulatory Issues: Ripple Labs is embroiled in a lawsuit with the U.S. Securities and Exchange Commission (SEC) alleging that XRP is an unregistered security.
- Impact: The legal uncertainty has led to delistings from major exchanges and has affected investor confidence.

7. Community and Development

Bitcoin (BTC)

- Community: Boasts a large and active community of developers, miners, and enthusiasts dedicated to its growth and security.
- Development: Focused on enhancing scalability and transaction efficiency through solutions like the Lightning Network.

XRP (Ripple)

- Community: Supported by Ripple Labs and a network of financial institutions. The broader community is smaller compared to Bitcoin's.
- Development: Continues to develop its ledger and partner with banks to improve international payment systems.

XRP or BTC

Choosing between XRP and BTC depends largely on your investment objectives and the use case you prioritize. Bitcoin stands out as the pioneering cryptocurrency, offering a decentralized and secure store of value with widespread adoption and recognition. It's often favored by investors seeking long-term growth and a hedge against traditional financial systems.

On the other hand, XRP excels in facilitating efficient and cost-effective cross-border transactions, making it an attractive option for financial institutions and those interested in the infrastructure side of cryptocurrencies. However, its centralization and ongoing legal challenges present both unique advantages and risks.

Ultimately, both cryptocurrencies have their merits and play distinct roles in the digital economy. Diversifying your portfolio to include both BTC and XRP could potentially offer a balanced exposure to both the investment and utility aspects of the cryptocurrency market.

X 12

12- XRP vs. Ethereum: Which One Is Better?

In the rapidly evolving landscape of cryptocurrencies, XRP and Ethereum stand out as two of the most prominent players. This article delves into the strengths and weaknesses of both cryptocurrencies, examining their use cases, technology, market performance, and overall potential. By the end, readers will have a clearer understanding of which asset may be better suited for their investment or utility needs.

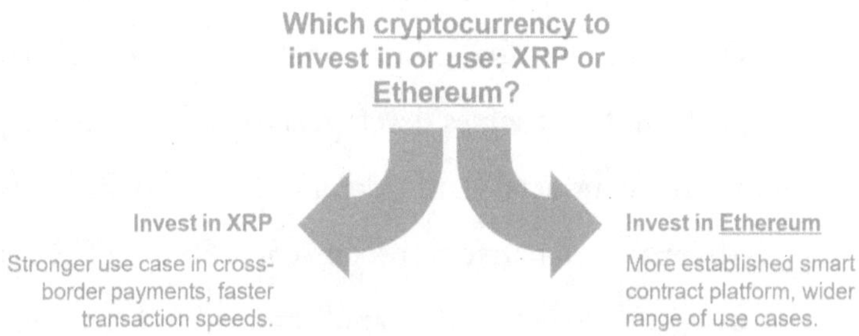

Overview of XRP and Ethereum

XRP

XRP is the native cryptocurrency of the Ripple network, designed primarily for facilitating cross-border payments and remittances. Ripple aims to provide a faster, more cost-effective alternative to traditional banking systems, enabling financial institutions to settle transactions in real-time. XRP's consensus algorithm allows for quick transaction confirmations, making it an attractive option for banks and payment providers.

Ethereum

Ethereum, on the other hand, is a decentralized platform that enables developers to build and deploy smart contracts and decentralized applications (dApps). Its native cryptocurrency, Ether (ETH), is used to power these applications and pay for transaction fees on the network. Ethereum's flexibility and programmability have made it the backbone of the decentralized finance (DeFi) ecosystem and non-fungible tokens (NFTs).

Use Cases

XRP Use Cases

1. Cross-Border Payments: XRP is primarily used for international money transfers, allowing for quick and low-cost transactions.

2. Liquidity Provision: Financial institutions can use XRP as a bridge currency to facilitate liquidity in various fiat currencies.

3. Partnerships with Banks: Ripple has established partnerships with numerous banks and financial institutions, enhancing its credibility and adoption.

Ethereum Use Cases

1. Smart Contracts: Ethereum's ability to execute self-executing contracts without intermediaries has revolutionized various industries.

2. Decentralized Finance (DeFi): Ethereum is the leading platform for DeFi applications, enabling users to lend, borrow, and trade assets without traditional financial intermediaries.

3. NFTs: Ethereum is the primary platform for creating and trading NFTs, which have gained immense popularity in the art and entertainment sectors.

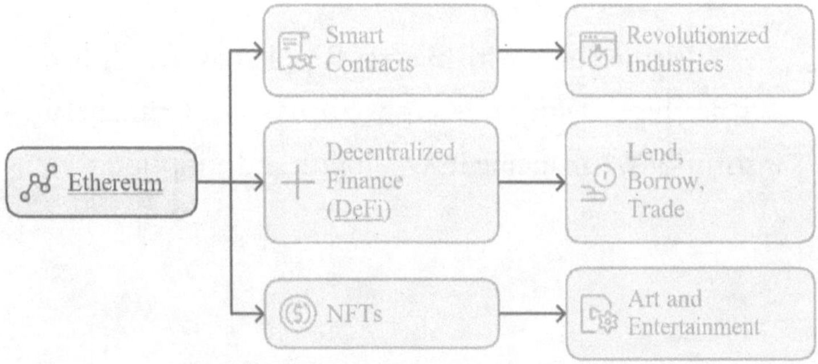

So, this battle offers two different points of view, both XRP and Ethereum offer distinct value propositions in the world of cryptocurrencies. XRP is primarily focused on facilitating fast, low-cost cross-border payments, making it a popular choice for financial institutions seeking efficient remittance solutions. On the other hand, Ethereum is a versatile platform for decentralized applications (dApps) and smart contracts, providing a robust infrastructure for various industries, including DeFi, NFTs, and more. While XRP excels in transaction speed and cost, Ethereum's extensive ecosystem and development flexibility make it a leader in blockchain innovation. The choice between the two ultimately depends on specific use cases and investment goals.

X 13

13-XRP and other Cryptocurrencies

Cryptocurrencies have revolutionized the way we think about financial transactions and investments. XRP, though not as universally recognized as Bitcoin or Ethereum, offers unique solutions within the realm of digital currencies. In the next pages we will have a detailed comparison of XRP with other leading cryptocurrencies, exploring its distinct position and potential in shaping the future of global transactions.

Comparing XRP with Top Cryptocurrencies

Here is how XRP stands alongside the ten most popular cryptocurrencies:

1. **Bitcoin (BTC)**: The original cryptocurrency, Bitcoin is primarily a digital gold and is used as a value store. XRP, on the other hand, excels in transactional efficiency with much lower fees and faster settlement times.

2. **Ethereum (ETH)**: As a platform for decentralized applications, Ethereum supports smart contracts. XRP does not offer smart contracts but has superior transaction throughput and lower fees, focusing on banking transactions.

3. **Binance Coin (BNB)**: Originally functioning within the Binance exchange ecosystem, BNB offers transaction fee discounts and other benefits within Binance. XRP's utility lies in its cross-border payment facilitation, which is more focused on institutional use.

4. **Cardano (ADA)**: Known for its research-backed approach and emphasis on security and sustainability, Cardano also supports smart contracts. XRP differs by not supporting decentralized applications, focusing instead on its role in fast, secure banking transactions.

5. **Solana (SOL)**: Praised for its high throughput and low fees, Solana supports decentralized applications and smart contracts. While similar in efficiency, XRP specializes in liquidity provision for fiat currencies in cross-border payments.

6. **Ripple (XRP)**: The centerpiece of this comparison, it boasts minimal transaction fees and maximum efficiency targeted towards financial institutions.

7. **Polkadot (DOT)**: It aims to enable different blockchains to transfer messages and value in a trust-free fashion; still, it's less tailored to the specific needs of the banking sector compared to XRP.

8. **Dogecoin (DOGE)**: Started as a meme, this coin has lower transaction costs but lacks the institutional focus that XRP has. Dogecoin is not widely used in business scenarios.

9. **Chainlink (LINK)**: As a decentralized oracle network, LINK provides real-world data to blockchains. XRP, unlike LINK, directly facilitates transactions and doesn't involve in smart contract data verification.

10. **Litecoin (LTC)**: Designed as "silver to Bitcoin's gold," Litecoin offers fast and relatively inexpensive transactions. It is more consumer-focused compared to XRP, which is tailored for high-frequency, large-scale institutional use.

The Unique Value Proposition of XRP

XRP's primary edge lies in its consensus protocol, offering rapid transaction settlements (3-5 seconds). This is coupled with low transaction costs, high scalability (1,500 transactions per second), and a design that addresses the needs of an essential market—international money transfers by banks.

Challenges and Future Prospects

Regulatory challenges, particularly the SEC's lawsuit in the U.S., have impacted XRP's reputation and use. However, its continued adoption by financial institutions and new partnerships in the banking sector could securely position XRP as a leader in financial blockchain solutions.

XRP in the Expanding World of Cryptocurrencies

In the fleetly expanding macrocosm of digital currencies, XRP stands out with its unique focus on reducing the disunion of transnational plutocrat transfers for banks and fiscal powers. Its future is tied not only to technological advancements but also to navigating the complex web of global regulations.

On the circle of invention, XRP is poised to become the autonomous of all cryptocurrencies and RWA, transforming global banking with unprecedented speed and effectiveness.

RWA: *Real World Assets; cryptocurrency tokens that represent physical goods that exist outside of the digital environment. These can include bonds, real estate properties, commodities, and machines.*

X 14

14-XRP and Central Banks: Friends or Foes?

What Are Central Banks?

Central banks are national institutions responsible for managing a country's currency, money supply, and interest rates. Their main goals are to control inflation, manage employment rates, and ensure financial stability. Examples include the Federal Reserve in the U.S., the European Central Bank (ECB), and the Bank of Japan (BOJ).

Central banks are critical to the functioning of the global financial system, holding reserves, issuing currency, and facilitating monetary policy. With the advent of cryptocurrencies, central banks face new challenges and opportunities, especially with the potential rise of Central Bank Digital Currencies (CBDCs). XRP, with its cross-border functionality, sits at the crossroads of this evolving financial landscape.

The Role of XRP in the Financial System

XRP was designed to address inefficiencies in cross-border payments, a space traditionally dominated by slow and expensive processes through intermediary banks. By acting as a bridge currency between different fiat currencies, XRP allows for near-instantaneous transactions with minimal costs. RippleNet, the network that utilizes XRP, enables financial institutions to transfer funds more quickly and efficiently than conventional systems like SWIFT.

The ability of XRP to settle transactions in just a few seconds, compared to the hours or even days that traditional methods take, makes it an attractive option for institutions. However, this speed and efficiency also challenge the status quo of central banks, which have historically controlled international transactions and liquidity.

Central Bank Digital Currencies (CBDCs) Explained

Central Bank Digital Currencies, or CBDCs, are digital versions of a country's fiat currency issued directly by the central bank. Unlike cryptocurrencies, which are decentralized, CBDCs are fully regulated and controlled by the central bank.

CBDCs offer central banks the ability to modernize payments, increase financial inclusion, and maintain control in an increasingly digital economy. Many countries, including China with its digital yuan and the European Union exploring the digital euro, are working towards developing their own CBDCs. In this context, XRP's cross-border utility intersects with the goals of CBDCs, but it also raises questions about whether they are competitors or collaborators.

How XRP and Ripple Connect to Central Banks

Ripple has actively sought partnerships with central banks, positioning XRP as a bridge asset for cross-border settlements. Through RippleNet, Ripple offers technology solutions that could complement CBDCs by allowing them to interact seamlessly with other currencies and financial systems.

For instance, Ripple has collaborated with central banks and financial institutions globally, including projects with the

Bank of England and several others in Asia and Latin America. These collaborations highlight Ripple's intention to work alongside central banks, rather than replace them. By providing liquidity and enabling faster transactions, XRP could serve as a valuable tool for central banks looking to enhance cross-border payment systems.

Potential Benefits of XRP to Central Banks

XRP offers several benefits to central banks that could foster a cooperative relationship:

- **Faster Settlements:** XRP's ability to process transactions in 3-5 seconds allows central banks to facilitate real-time cross-border payments, reducing delays and costs associated with traditional systems.
- **Lower Transaction Costs:** XRP's low transaction fees are advantageous for central banks and financial institutions aiming to lower operational costs, especially in remittances and international settlements.
- **Liquidity Provision:** XRP can act as a bridge currency, providing liquidity between different fiat currencies and reducing the need for pre-funded nostro accounts.
- **Interoperability with Existing Systems:** Ripple's solutions are designed to integrate with existing financial

infrastructures, making it easier for central banks to adopt without overhauling their systems.

Challenges and Risks of XRP for Central Banks

Despite its benefits, there are potential challenges and risks for central banks in adopting or integrating XRP into their systems:

- **Regulatory Concerns:** XRP has faced significant regulatory scrutiny, particularly in the U.S., where the SEC has filed a lawsuit against Ripple, claiming that XRP is an unregistered security. Regulatory uncertainty could deter central banks from fully embracing the technology.
- **Control Over Monetary Policy:** Central banks may view XRP as a threat to their control over monetary policy, especially if XRP or other cryptocurrencies gain widespread adoption. This decentralization could undermine the traditional role of central banks in controlling money supply and interest rates.
- **Security Risks:** Like all digital assets, XRP and its infrastructure are susceptible to cyberattacks and hacking, which could pose risks to financial stability if central banks rely on such systems for cross-border payments.

The Role of Regulation in the XRP-Central Bank Relationship

Regulation is a critical factor in determining the future relationship between XRP and central banks. Governments and central banks are increasingly focusing on regulating cryptocurrencies to ensure financial stability and protect consumers.

For XRP to gain widespread acceptance among central banks, it must comply with regulatory frameworks that govern financial institutions. Ripple has expressed its willingness to work with regulators to ensure compliance, and several countries have already implemented or are in the process of developing regulatory frameworks for cryptocurrencies.

XRP vs. Traditional Cross-Border Payments

Traditional cross-border payment systems, such as SWIFT, are often criticized for being slow and expensive. Transfers can take days to process, and transaction fees are high, especially for smaller amounts. XRP offers a more efficient alternative with faster settlement times and lower costs.

However, SWIFT has been a trusted system for decades, and central banks may be reluctant to switch entirely to a new, relatively untested system like XRP. Yet, as RippleNet continues to grow, central banks could increasingly see the value in adopting XRP as part of a hybrid approach to cross-border payments.

Central Bank Digital Currencies (CBDCs) vs. XRP

CBDCs and XRP could coexist in the financial ecosystem, serving different roles. While CBDCs would be state-issued and controlled by central banks, XRP could act as a bridge currency, facilitating the exchange of CBDCs across borders.

Some experts believe that the rise of CBDCs could marginalize cryptocurrencies like XRP, while others argue that Ripple's technology could enhance the functionality of CBDCs by providing liquidity and interoperability.

Global Partnerships and Collaborations with Central Banks

Ripple has made significant strides in partnering with central banks and financial institutions globally. From the Monetary Authority of Singapore to central banks in the Middle East, Ripple has worked to position its technology as a complement to existing financial systems.

These partnerships reflect Ripple's strategy to integrate with, rather than replace, central banks, fostering a symbiotic relationship that could benefit both parties in the long run.

Criticisms of XRP: A Centralized Cryptocurrency?

One of the major criticisms of XRP is its perceived centralization. Unlike Bitcoin, which is fully decentralized, a large portion of XRP's supply is held by Ripple Labs. Critics argue that this concentration of ownership gives Ripple undue control over the XRP network, making it more akin to a centralized entity than a decentralized cryptocurrency.

This criticism is particularly important for central banks, which may be wary of adopting a digital asset that is not fully decentralized. Ripple has countered these claims, emphasizing that XRP operates on an open-source ledger and is not controlled by any single entity.

Future Outlook: Can XRP Coexist with CBDCs?

The future of XRP in the context of central banks largely depends on how CBDCs develop and how Ripple continues to position its technology. If CBDCs become widely adopted, XRP could play a crucial role in enabling cross-border transactions between different digital currencies.

Moreover, as central banks continue to explore blockchain technology, Ripple's solutions could help bridge the gap between traditional financial systems and the new digital economy. The key will be how Ripple navigates regulatory challenges and continues to foster partnerships with central banks.

Case Studies: Central Banks Utilizing Ripple's Technology

Several central banks have already tested or adopted Ripple's technology. For example:

- **The Bank of England** worked with Ripple on a proof of concept for cross-border payments.
- **The Monetary Authority of Singapore** has explored Ripple's solutions as part of its blockchain initiative.

- **The Saudi Arabian Monetary Authority (SAMA)** partnered with Ripple to provide pilot programs for cross-border transactions.

These case studies demonstrate that while central banks may not fully embrace XRP, they are open to using Ripple's technology to improve their payment systems.

Are Central Banks and XRP Allies or Adversaries?

XRP has the potential to become a valuable ally for central banks by serving as a bridge currency for international transactions. Its speed, low costs, and ability to provide liquidity between different fiat currencies make it an attractive solution for central banks seeking to modernize cross-border payments. By leveraging XRP, central banks can achieve faster, safer, and more efficient global transactions, streamlining their operations without compromising control over their national currencies. As the financial landscape continues to evolve, XRP could play a key role in bridging traditional banking systems with the future of digital finance.

X 15

15-How XRP price is determined

The price of any cryptocurrency, including XRP, is a complex phenomenon influenced by a multitude of factors, both internal and external to the market. XRP, the native digital asset of the Ripple network, plays a crucial role in facilitating fast, low-cost international transactions. But how exactly is its price determined? This article provides a deep dive into the mechanics behind XRP's valuation, analyzing the interplay of various forces such as market demand, supply, technological advancements, regulatory influences, and broader economic trends.

1. Overview of XRP and Ripple: The Foundation

To understand how XRP's price is determined, it's essential to grasp what XRP is and how it functions within the broader Ripple ecosystem.

Ripple, the company behind XRP, is a blockchain-based payment protocol designed to make cross-border transactions faster and more efficient. Unlike Bitcoin or Ethereum, which focus on decentralized finance and smart contracts, Ripple aims to serve financial institutions with its RippleNet platform, using XRP as a bridge currency for liquidity. XRP transactions are confirmed in seconds and at minimal cost, making it an attractive option for banks and payment providers looking for cross-border payment solutions.

However, despite Ripple's prominence in the financial sector, XRP's price is influenced by a variety of factors, some unique to its ecosystem and others shared with the broader cryptocurrency market.

2. Supply and Demand: The Core Price Drivers

Like any other asset, XRP's price is subject to the fundamental economic principle of supply and demand. If demand exceeds supply, the price rises; conversely, if supply outstrips demand, the price drops. For XRP, both supply and demand are influenced by several unique factors:

a. Total Supply of XRP

XRP has a capped total supply of 100 billion coins, of which a significant portion is held by Ripple Labs, the company that developed the Ripple payment protocol. This large reserve has sparked debates about centralization concerns, as Ripple Labs can release XRP from escrow at strategic intervals, influencing market supply.

Ripple typically releases around 1 billion XRP tokens each month, but not all of these tokens necessarily enter circulation. Any unsold XRP is placed back into escrow, ensuring that supply remains somewhat controlled. This escrow mechanism helps maintain market stability and prevents oversupply from diluting XRP's value.

b. Market Demand for XRP

XRP's utility in international payments creates real-world demand. Ripple's partnerships with financial institutions, payment processors, and remittance companies drive demand for XRP as a liquidity bridge for cross-border transactions. As Ripple's network expands, more institutions may adopt XRP for transaction settlements, increasing demand.

In addition to institutional demand, retail investors play a significant role. As interest in cryptocurrencies grows, many see XRP as a speculative investment, increasing demand from individual traders and investors.

3. Liquidity and Market Sentiment

Liquidity refers to the ease with which an asset can be bought or sold without affecting its price. High liquidity often leads to less volatility, while low liquidity can result in price swings. For XRP, liquidity is influenced by its presence on major cryptocurrency exchanges and the volume of trading activity.

Market sentiment also plays a crucial role in XRP's price movements. Positive news, such as Ripple securing partnerships with major financial institutions or regulatory clarity on XRP's status as a currency rather than a security, can lead to price increases. On the flip side, negative news, such as the lawsuit filed by the U.S. Securities and Exchange Commission (SEC) in 2020, can cause significant price declines. The outcome of this lawsuit, which challenges whether XRP should be classified as a security, continues to influence market sentiment and thus, XRP's price.

4. External Market Factors: Impact of Bitcoin and Overall Cryptocurrency Market

The price of XRP is also influenced by broader cryptocurrency market trends. Historically, most altcoins, including XRP, have shown a strong correlation with Bitcoin's price. When Bitcoin rises, altcoins tend to follow, and when Bitcoin falls, the altcoin market often declines in tandem.

This correlation is partly due to Bitcoin's dominant position in the market as the first and most widely recognized cryptocurrency. Investors often view Bitcoin as a gateway to the cryptocurrency world, meaning market-wide price movements are often driven by shifts in Bitcoin's value.

However, while XRP's price movements may be correlated with Bitcoin, it still retains its own unique drivers due to its specific use cases and institutional adoption through Ripple's payment network.

5. Technological Developments: Ripple Network and XRP's Use Case

Technological advancements and updates in the Ripple network can have a direct impact on XRP's price. If Ripple introduces new features or upgrades that enhance the utility or efficiency of XRP in cross-border transactions, this can attract more users to the network, boosting demand for XRP.

Additionally, any technological developments that improve scalability, transaction speed, or cost efficiency will make XRP more attractive to financial institutions. The greater the adoption of XRP in real-world financial transactions, the higher the demand, which can push the price upwards.

Ripple's ODL (On-Demand Liquidity) Solution

One of the key technological drivers for XRP's demand is Ripple's On-Demand Liquidity (ODL) product. ODL uses XRP to provide liquidity for cross-border payments, eliminating the need for pre-funded nostro accounts. As more financial institutions adopt ODL, demand for XRP as a liquidity tool increases, potentially driving up its price.

6. Regulatory Environment: A Crucial Influence

One of the most significant factors influencing XRP's price is the regulatory environment, particularly in the United States. The ongoing SEC lawsuit, which alleges that XRP is a security and not a currency, has created uncertainty around the asset. This uncertainty has caused price volatility, as many investors wait for a clear regulatory ruling.

In countries with clear regulatory frameworks, XRP adoption has been more straightforward, and this clarity often translates into price stability or growth. Conversely, regulatory crackdowns or bans on cryptocurrency use in major markets can have a negative impact on XRP's price.

The SEC Lawsuit and Its Implications

The SEC lawsuit against Ripple, filed in December 2020, has been a pivotal event in determining XRP's price trajectory. The lawsuit claimed that Ripple conducted an unregistered securities offering by selling XRP. This legal battle has impacted XRP's availability on U.S. exchanges and cast a shadow of uncertainty over its future.

A positive outcome for Ripple could lead to a sharp increase in XRP's price, as it would remove the regulatory overhang that has deterred some investors. Conversely, a negative ruling could result in further price declines or delisting from exchanges that operate in jurisdictions with stringent securities laws.

7. Market Speculation and Whale Activity

Like many other cryptocurrencies, XRP's price can be influenced by speculative trading. Speculators often buy and sell XRP based on short-term price movements, creating volatility. The presence of "whales," or large holders of XRP, can also lead to sudden price fluctuations if they decide to sell or move significant quantities of XRP.

Whales, including institutional investors and early adopters who hold large amounts of XRP, can influence the market by liquidating their holdings or purchasing more XRP in large quantities. This creates significant price swings that may not necessarily reflect the fundamental value of the asset.

8. Global Economic Trends and External Market Conditions

The price of XRP, like other cryptocurrencies, is influenced by broader economic trends. Global financial instability, inflation concerns, or interest rate hikes can lead investors to seek alternative assets like cryptocurrencies.

Conversely, periods of economic stability and growth may see a reduced interest in cryptocurrencies as investors gravitate towards traditional financial instruments.

Additionally, as XRP is often viewed as a bridge currency in cross-border payments, global trade dynamics and economic partnerships can influence its demand and price.

Frequently Asked Questions (FAQs)

1. Does Ripple control XRP's price?

Ripple has significant control over the supply of XRP through its escrow mechanism, but it doesn't directly control the market price. XRP's price is influenced by demand from market participants, traders, and institutional users.

2. What impact does the SEC lawsuit have on XRP's price?

The SEC lawsuit has created uncertainty around XRP's regulatory status, leading to price volatility. A favorable outcome could lead to price increases, while an unfavorable ruling might negatively impact the price.

3. How does Bitcoin's price affect XRP?

XRP's price often follows broader cryptocurrency market trends, which are heavily influenced by Bitcoin. When

Bitcoin's price rises, XRP usually sees upward movement, and vice versa.

4. What role does supply and demand play in XRP's price?

Supply and demand are fundamental factors. If demand for XRP increases, for example, through institutional adoption, the price may rise. Conversely, if supply outpaces demand, the price may fall.

5. Can technological advancements in RippleNet affect XRP's price?

Yes, innovations like Ripple's On-Demand Liquidity (ODL) system can drive demand for XRP, potentially raising its price as more institutions adopt these technologies for cross-border payments.

6. Is XRP's price likely to stabilize in the future?

While XRP's price will likely remain volatile in the near term due to ongoing legal and regulatory issues, greater institutional adoption and regulatory clarity could stabilize the price over time.

How will the price XRP work?

The value of XRP is calculated by dividing the ledger's value-volume ratio by the circulating supply. It is not easy to determine the circulating supply. The circulating supply of XRP is approximately 56.64 billion. This number is deceptive.

Just because 56.6 billion exists, doesn't mean all of it is available for use on the XRP ledger. The majority of those funds are stored in personal wallets, owned by individuals, or kept in cryptocurrency exchanges. The price is determined by the amount of supply that is actively present on the ledger. My estimate is that approximately 15% of it is actively used on the ledger every day. For the purposes of this example, let's assume that nearly 10 billion is in the AMM pools paired with either XRP or RLUSD. The banks and financial institutions will possess their individual tokens or CBDC's. They will match those holding RLUSD and conduct transactions utilizing the liquidity available in the AMM pools.

The XRPL is equipped with an algorithm that looks for the optimal method to ensure liquidity for finalizing a transaction. This algorithm relies on XRP as the primary settlement source and will only switch to an alternative if it proves to be more effective than XRP. It is improbable that this will happen. To provide an illustration of the potential value/volume on the ledger: Sift handles around $6 trillion in daily settlements, J.P. Morgan handles $9 trillion, Bank of America handles approximately $8 trillion, and SBI Japan handles $2 trillion. Around $25 trillion is settled daily with only four banks or institutions involved. Ripple has more than 1700 non-disclosure agreements, of which only a small portion are known to us. Let's select only 10% of the total amount, which is $2.5 trillion, and allocate it to the ledger for use in AMM pools.

These pools need to be roughly twice the value of $2.5 trillion to prevent unsuccessful transactions and conflicts within the pools. Banks are unable to have unsuccessful transactions. Therefore, the actual amount recorded on the ledger must be approximately $5 trillion. In order to ensure smooth transactions between various currencies or CBDC's, the price of XRP should be such that it creates deep liquidity pools and avoids any friction. This calculation involves dividing the $5 trillion by the 10 billion XRP in the pools. For settlement to occur daily, the price of XRP would have to reach approx $500 or more. This is a simple demonstration of the potential outcome when these banks begin utilizing XRP regularly for settlements. Tokenized assets, tokenized debt, and tokenized real estate, among other factors, will contribute value to the ledger in the future. If you believe XRP will never have a high value, it shows you lack understanding of its future use and function.

Retail is irrelevant, market cap is inconsequential, and charts are merely aesthetically pleasing but also irrelevant. It is impossible to predict the amount of liquidity/depth of AMM Pools required to process the settlement of over 1700 NDA's daily. No one knows the exact magnitude of that number. XRP needs to maintain a high price in order to effectively carry out its intended purpose of processing large transactions quickly and affordably.

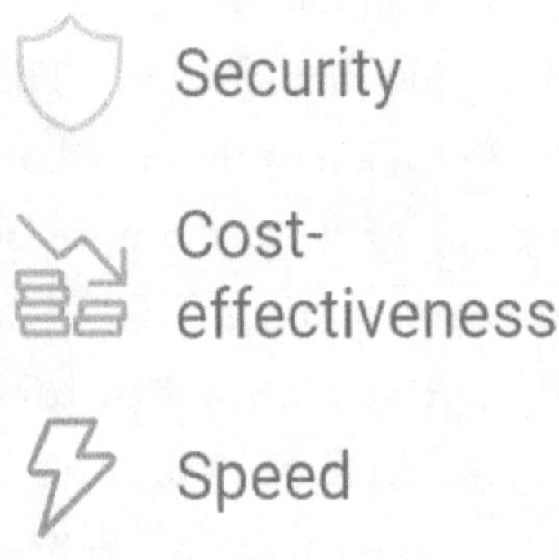

3 values to conquest the world

X 16

16-XRP and the Future of Remittances

Benefits of Using XRP for Remittances

XRP offers a number of advantages for both senders and receivers in the remittance process:

- **Cost savings:** Lower transaction fees mean more money is received by the recipient, which is crucial for families relying on remittances as a primary source of income.
- **Speed:** Faster transaction times ensure that funds are available to recipients immediately, which can be essential in emergency situations.
- **Transparency:** All transactions on the XRP Ledger are recorded on a public ledger, providing transparency and reducing the risk of fraud or error.
- **Accessibility:** XRP can be sent and received by anyone with an internet connection, breaking down barriers for unbanked populations in remote or underdeveloped areas.

1. XRP vs. Traditional Remittance Methods

When comparing XRP to traditional remittance methods, the differences are stark:

Feature	XRP	Traditional Remittance Methods
Transaction Speed	3-5 seconds	1-5 days
Fees	Less than $0.01	5-10%
Transparency	Public ledger	Limited
Intermediaries	None	Multiple
Accessibility	Global, borderless	Limited to banked populations

2. Real-World Use Cases of XRP in Remittances

Several companies and financial institutions have already begun adopting XRP to improve their remittance services. Ripple's On-Demand Liquidity (ODL) has been deployed by major remittance companies such as:

- **MoneyGram:** One of the largest remittance providers globally, MoneyGram partnered with Ripple to use XRP for instant cross-border settlements, significantly reducing transaction costs and settlement times.
- **SBI Remit:** A subsidiary of the Japanese financial giant SBI Holdings, SBI Remit uses XRP to streamline international money transfers between Japan and Southeast Asia, providing faster and cheaper services.

These partnerships demonstrate how XRP is already making a tangible impact on the remittance industry.

3. Adoption of XRP by Financial Institutions

One of the most promising aspects of XRP is its growing adoption by mainstream financial institutions. Banks and payment providers are beginning to recognize the benefits of blockchain technology for improving the speed and efficiency of cross-border transactions.

Ripple has formed partnerships with over 300 financial institutions globally, including Santander, Standard Chartered, and American Express. These partnerships aim to leverage XRP and Ripple's technology to enhance the global payment infrastructure.

4. XRP and the Regulatory Environment

While XRP holds tremendous potential for revolutionizing remittances, it also faces challenges in terms of regulation. Many governments are still developing frameworks to govern digital currencies and blockchain-based payment systems.

In the United States, Ripple has been embroiled in legal disputes with the Securities and Exchange Commission (SEC) over whether XRP should be classified as a security. The outcome of this case could have significant implications for the future of XRP in the remittance industry.

5. How Ripple's On-Demand Liquidity (ODL) is Changing Remittances

Ripple's On-Demand Liquidity (ODL) uses XRP to bridge different currencies in real-time, eliminating the need for pre-funded accounts in different countries. This drastically reduces the capital required by financial institutions to facilitate cross-border payments.

For example, a financial institution in the United States can use ODL to convert USD into XRP, send the XRP to Mexico, and convert it into Mexican pesos instantly. This process takes seconds and incurs minimal fees, making it a game-changer for remittance companies.

6. Potential Roadblocks to XRP Adoption in the Remittance Space

Despite the advantages XRP offers, there are several challenges to its widespread adoption in the remittance industry:

- **Regulatory uncertainty:** The regulatory status of digital assets like XRP varies widely across different jurisdictions, creating challenges for global adoption.

- **Volatility:** Like all cryptocurrencies, XRP's value can fluctuate significantly, which may pose a risk for users who want stable, predictable transfers.
- **Competition:** XRP is not the only digital asset aiming to disrupt the remittance market. Cryptocurrencies like Bitcoin, Ethereum, and stablecoins also offer alternatives, each with its own strengths and weaknesses.

7. The Role of XRP in Financial Inclusion

One of the most promising aspects of XRP is its potential to improve financial inclusion. Over 1.7 billion people globally are unbanked, meaning they lack access to basic financial services. XRP's borderless, low-cost, and accessible nature makes it an ideal solution for extending financial services to underserved populations.

By reducing the cost of remittances and increasing access to financial tools, XRP could help lift millions of people out of poverty by providing them with the means to participate in the global economy.

X 17

17-XRP and the Future of Micropayments

---

1. How XRP Revolutionizes Micropayments

Micropayments, though potentially transformative, have struggled to gain traction within traditional financial systems due to high transaction fees and slow settlement times. Even for online platforms like PayPal or Stripe, processing fees can eat up a significant portion of a small transaction, often making them impractical for regular use. The same issues extend to credit card payments, where flat fees make micropayments infeasible for both merchants and consumers.

This is where **XRP** and the **XRP Ledger** shine.

XRP's blockchain-based network offers several advantages that solve these issues:

- **Speed:** Transactions on the XRP Ledger are settled in 3-5 seconds, allowing micropayments to be processed nearly instantaneously.
- **Low fees:** With an average transaction fee of less than $0.01, XRP makes it financially viable to send payments of even a few cents. This is crucial for micropayments, where minimizing costs is essential.
- **Scalability:** The XRP Ledger can handle up to 1,500 transactions per second, ensuring that the network can handle a high volume of small-value transactions without bottlenecks.

These characteristics make XRP an ideal candidate for powering a broad range of digital micropayments, from tipping content creators online to paying for individual services in decentralized apps (dApps).

2. Benefits of Using XRP for Micropayments

The advantages of using XRP for micropayments go beyond speed and cost-effectiveness. Here are a few key benefits:

- **Increased transaction efficiency:** With no need for intermediaries like banks or payment processors, XRP enables direct peer-to-peer transactions, cutting out unnecessary steps and reducing overhead costs.

- **Enhanced accessibility:** XRP can be used globally, facilitating micropayments across borders without the need for currency conversions or excessive foreign exchange fees.
- **Microtransaction support:** The XRP Ledger's design allows for the creation of payments as small as fractions of a cent, enabling use cases that are simply not possible with traditional payment systems.
- **Security and transparency:** As a decentralized blockchain, the XRP Ledger offers built-in security through its cryptographic protocols. Each transaction is recorded on a public ledger, ensuring transparency and accountability.

These features position XRP as a viable solution for industries looking to implement efficient and reliable micropayment systems.

3. XRP and the Streaming Economy

One of the most promising applications for XRP in the micropayments space lies in the **streaming economy**, particularly in sectors like media, music, and gaming. The rise of streaming services has transformed how consumers access digital content, and XRP could play a pivotal role in enhancing these services by enabling frictionless, pay-per-use models.

Consider the following examples:

- **Streaming media and music:** Instead of subscribing to a service for a flat monthly fee, users could pay for individual songs, videos, or media content on a per-second or per-minute basis. With XRP, microtransactions can occur seamlessly in real time, ensuring that consumers only pay for what they consume.
- **Online gaming:** The gaming industry could implement XRP micropayments to power in-game purchases, tipping systems, or even peer-to-peer bets. This would eliminate the need for third-party payment processors, reducing fees and improving the user experience.
- **Tipping for content creators:** Platforms like YouTube, Twitch, or independent blogs could use XRP to facilitate micropayments from viewers. Users could tip creators small amounts of XRP, making it easier for creators to monetize their content without relying on advertisements or large subscription fees.

By reducing the friction associated with small payments, XRP enables a more fluid and dynamic exchange of value in the digital world, allowing content creators, service providers, and consumers to engage in new ways.

4. Use Cases for XRP in Micropayments

The use cases for XRP in the micropayment space are numerous and varied, spanning across different industries and sectors. Here are some key examples:

- **Pay-per-article journalism:** Instead of subscribing to an entire publication, users could pay a few cents to access individual articles on demand. This model could open up new monetization strategies for independent writers and smaller media outlets.
- **IoT payments:** In the **Internet of Things (IoT)** space, devices can transact with one another using micropayments. For example, a smart car could pay for road tolls, parking meters, or even electric charging on a per-minute or per-use basis using XRP.
- **Decentralized applications (dApps):** dApps built on blockchain technology can use XRP to facilitate small payments for services such as file storage, computing power, or digital identity verification.
- **E-commerce:** Online platforms could enable shoppers to make micropayments for virtual goods, digital downloads, or trial versions of software without incurring hefty processing fees.

These examples illustrate how XRP could transform various sectors by reducing the costs and inefficiencies associated with processing small payments.

5. Comparing XRP to Other Micropayment Solutions

XRP is not the only digital asset vying for dominance in the micropayment space. However, it holds several distinct advantages over other cryptocurrencies and traditional payment systems.

- **Bitcoin:** While Bitcoin is the most widely recognized cryptocurrency, its slow transaction times (averaging 10 minutes per block) and high fees make it impractical for micropayments. The Bitcoin Lightning Network has attempted to address these issues, but it remains less efficient than XRP's core system.
- **Ethereum:** Ethereum offers faster transaction times than Bitcoin, but it struggles with network congestion and high gas fees, particularly during periods of heavy usage. This makes it a less suitable option for consistent, low-cost micropayments.
- **Stablecoins (e.g., USDC, DAI):** Stablecoins offer the benefit of price stability, but they are often built on networks with similar scalability and fee challenges as Ethereum. XRP's

low fees and high throughput make it a more efficient choice for micropayments.

When compared to traditional financial systems, XRP's advantages are even more pronounced. Payment processors like Visa and Mastercard typically charge a minimum flat fee, which can consume a significant percentage of a small transaction's value. This makes them unsuitable for true micropayments.

6. Challenges to XRP Adoption in Micropayments

Despite its potential, XRP faces several challenges in achieving widespread adoption for micropayments:

- **Regulatory hurdles:** XRP's legal status, particularly in the United States, remains unclear due to ongoing disputes with regulators. This uncertainty may hinder some businesses and platforms from adopting XRP in the short term.
- **Market volatility:** As with most cryptocurrencies, XRP's value can fluctuate, which poses a risk for micropayment systems where users need price stability. However, solutions such as pegging XRP to stablecoins or fiat currencies in real-time conversions could mitigate this risk.
- **Competing technologies:** XRP is not the only blockchain offering fast, low-cost transactions. Competitors like Stellar (XLM) also target the micropayment space, and

the rise of **Layer 2** solutions on Ethereum could provide viable alternatives.

Despite these challenges, XRP's core attributes—speed, scalability, and low transaction costs—position it as a strong contender for powering the future of micropayments.

7. The Role of XRP in Content Monetization

As online content consumption continues to grow, creators are searching for new ways to monetize their work without relying solely on advertising or platform-dependent revenue models. XRP presents a solution through **direct micropayments**, allowing creators to bypass intermediaries and earn revenue directly from their audience.

For example:

- **Bloggers and writers** could integrate XRP micropayments into their websites, enabling readers to pay small amounts for access to premium content or to support their favorite authors through tipping.
- **Video creators** could implement a pay-per-view model where viewers pay a fraction of a dollar for exclusive videos or tutorials.

- **Artists and musicians** could use XRP to sell digital art, music tracks, or other forms of creative work directly to fans without incurring high platform fees.

This decentralized approach to content monetization empowers creators to take control of their earnings and engage more directly with their audiences.

8. Financial Inclusion and the Power of Micropayments

Beyond just facilitating new business models, micropayments powered by XRP could have a significant impact on **financial inclusion**. Around the world, millions of people remain excluded from traditional banking systems, making it difficult for them to participate in the global economy.

XRP, with its low fees and ease of use, offers a solution for underserved populations:

- **Access to financial services:** Individuals in developing countries can use XRP to make microloans, pay for services, or receive remittances, even without a formal bank account.
- **Participation in the digital economy:** By enabling micropayments, XRP can help more people engage in online commerce, pay for digital goods and services, and earn an income in new and innovative ways.

In this sense, XRP not only transforms digital payments but also contributes to greater financial inclusion worldwide.

9. The Future of Micropayments with XRP

The future of micropayments is set to be reshaped by blockchain technology, and XRP stands at the forefront of this revolution. By providing a fast, secure, and cost-effective way to transfer small amounts of value, XRP opens up new possibilities for digital commerce, content monetization, and financial inclusion.

As adoption grows and regulatory hurdles are addressed, we can expect to see XRP powering an increasing number of micropayment applications, from pay-per-use services to peer-to-peer financial transactions. Ultimately, XRP could play a pivotal role in creating a more efficient, inclusive, and interconnected global economy.

X 18

18-XRP and the Future of E-commerce

XRP is increasingly seen as a significant player in the future of e-commerce due to its ability to streamline cross-border payments, reduce transaction costs, and enhance financial inclusivity. Ripple's technology is designed to enable faster, more efficient, and less costly transfers of value across borders, making it an attractive option for businesses operating in the global digital marketplace.

The Role of XRP in E-commerce

XRP aims to solve one of the biggest challenges in e-commerce: cross-border payments. Traditional payment systems can be slow and expensive, particularly when transferring money between different countries. With its ability to settle transactions almost instantaneously at a fraction of the cost of traditional methods, XRP offers a more efficient alternative to systems like SWIFT.

For businesses, especially small and medium enterprises (SMEs), XRP could reduce reliance on intermediaries like banks or third-party payment processors, thereby lowering fees and improving profit margins. The use of RippleNet, Ripple's decentralized financial technology, can enable businesses to operate seamlessly across borders without the friction typically associated with international payments.

XRP's Benefits for E-commerce Growth

1. **Speed**: Ripple's ledger can settle payments in mere seconds, compared to the hours or even days required by traditional banking systems. This is critical for e-commerce businesses that operate globally, as faster payments enable quicker processing of orders and improve cash flow management.
2. **Lower Costs**: XRP's transaction fees are minimal compared to traditional banking and payment systems. This is especially relevant in cross-border e-commerce, where businesses typically face high foreign exchange costs and transaction fees.
3. **Scalability and Accessibility**: Ripple's blockchain technology is highly scalable, capable of handling thousands of transactions per second. Moreover, XRP's use in e-commerce could increase financial inclusion by providing a

low-cost alternative for businesses and consumers in regions with limited access to traditional banking services.

The Future of E-commerce with XRP

As e-commerce continues to expand globally, particularly in emerging markets, XRP could play a critical role in democratizing access to fast and affordable financial services. Its decentralized nature allows for greater transparency and security, key considerations in an increasingly digital economy.

Additionally, Ripple's partnerships with major financial institutions could help integrate XRP more seamlessly into global payment systems, further encouraging adoption within the e-commerce sector. As the demand for quicker, cheaper, and more secure online transactions grows, XRP is positioned to become a critical tool for e-commerce businesses looking to streamline operations and expand globally.

Challenges and Regulatory Considerations

However, XRP's future in e-commerce is not without challenges. Ripple has faced legal scrutiny from regulators like the U.S. Securities and Exchange Commission (SEC), which has argued that XRP is a security and not just a currency. The outcome of this legal dispute could significantly impact XRP's adoption and use in commerce, particularly in the U.S. market.

In conclusion, XRP has the potential to revolutionize the future of e-commerce by providing faster, cheaper, and more inclusive payment solutions. However, regulatory clarity and adoption by more e-commerce platforms will be crucial for its long-term success.

X 19

19-XRP and the Future of Gaming

As the gaming industry evolves into a multi-billion-dollar ecosystem, digital currencies like XRP are poised to transform the landscape. XRP, Ripple's native cryptocurrency, offers fast, low-cost transactions, making it an attractive solution for in-game purchases, microtransactions, and cross-border payments in the gaming world. With blockchain technology becoming more integrated into gaming platforms, XRP stands out as a currency that can address current challenges related to payment processing, fraud, and accessibility, while also creating new possibilities for player rewards and decentralized gaming economies.

XRP's Role in the Gaming Industry

1. **Microtransactions and In-Game Purchases**: In the current gaming economy, microtransactions are a key revenue stream, allowing players to purchase virtual goods, skins, or upgrades. However, traditional payment systems often come with high fees and slow processing times,

especially for international transactions. XRP's low transaction costs and near-instant settlements offer a frictionless alternative, enabling developers and gamers to process small payments quickly and affordably. This is particularly important for freemium models and games with real-money transactions.

2. **Decentralized Gaming Economies**: As more games adopt blockchain-based models, decentralized economies are becoming integral to the gaming experience. In these models, in-game assets, currencies, and rewards are often tokenized and can be traded both within the game and on external markets. XRP's scalability and liquidity make it an ideal digital currency to serve as a bridge between various gaming tokens and real-world currencies, facilitating seamless trading and asset transfers. This helps create more robust and interoperable gaming ecosystems.

3. **Cross-Border Payments and Accessibility**: With gaming's massive global audience, cross-border payments have traditionally posed challenges due to currency exchange fees, delays, and regulatory issues. XRP can remove these barriers by enabling fast, secure, and low-cost international transactions, making it easier for players around the world to engage with their favorite games. This could be a game-changer for gamers in regions with limited access to traditional banking systems, where XRP could offer an

inclusive and accessible way to participate in the global gaming economy.

Enhancing Gaming with Blockchain and XRP

1. **NFTs and Virtual Asset Ownership**: Non-fungible tokens (NFTs) are becoming increasingly popular in gaming, offering players true ownership of in-game assets like characters, weapons, and real estate. XRP's blockchain can support the tokenization of these assets, enabling secure, verifiable ownership. By integrating XRP, developers can enhance player trust, as ownership of rare items or collectibles can be traded on a decentralized ledger that ensures transparency and security.
2. **Esports and Tournament Payments**: Esports, one of the fastest-growing segments of the gaming industry, often involves players and teams from different countries competing for prize pools. XRP's ability to facilitate instant cross-border payments makes it an ideal currency for disbursing tournament winnings, sponsorship money, and other financial rewards. This could streamline the often complex payment structures in esports, improving financial inclusivity for players and organizations across the globe.
3. **Smart Contracts for Transparent Gaming**: XRP's underlying technology, Ripple's blockchain, can also support smart contracts, enabling automated and transparent transactions in gaming. For example, in a decentralized gaming marketplace, smart contracts could be used to ensure that

payments are automatically executed once specific conditions are met—such as the delivery of a virtual good or the completion of a gaming milestone. This would reduce fraud, eliminate the need for third-party intermediaries, and build trust among players and developers.

XRP and the Metaverse

As the concept of the metaverse gains traction, XRP could play a significant role in facilitating digital economies within these virtual worlds. The metaverse, envisioned as a fully immersive online environment, will require a stable, scalable, and interoperable payment system for transactions between users, creators, and businesses. XRP's speed, low fees, and cross-border functionality make it a strong candidate for powering financial interactions in this interconnected digital universe. By leveraging XRP, users in the metaverse could easily purchase digital goods, real estate, or services, regardless of their geographic location.

Challenges and Regulatory Considerations

Despite XRP's potential to reshape the future of gaming, regulatory challenges remain. Ripple's ongoing legal battle with the U.S. Securities and Exchange Commission (SEC), which claims that XRP is an unregistered security, could impact the token's adoption in gaming. The outcome of this case will influence how XRP is regulated and whether it can be freely used by gaming platforms, particularly in the U.S. market.

XRP and the Future of Gaming: Revolutionizing In-Game Payments and Microtransactions

XRP's unique advantages—such as fast, low-cost payments, scalability, and the ability to support decentralized economies—position it as a key player in the future of gaming. By integrating XRP, developers can unlock new opportunities for microtransactions, enhance player engagement through real asset ownership, and create more inclusive global gaming communities. While regulatory hurdles need to be addressed, the potential for XRP to transform the gaming industry is vast, particularly as gaming continues to merge with blockchain technology and the metaverse. As these trends evolve, XRP could become a cornerstone of the digital payment infrastructure in gaming's next era.

Jon Erlaitz

X 20

20-XRP and the Future of Social Media

As social media continues to evolve into a central hub for communication, content creation, and commerce, integrating blockchain technology and digital currencies like XRP could significantly reshape how these platforms operate. XRP, known for its fast, low-cost transactions, presents unique opportunities for social media users, content creators, and businesses alike. With the potential to streamline payments, enable microtransactions, and facilitate decentralized content ecosystems, XRP is well-positioned to play a key role in the future of social media.

XRP in Social Media Payments

1. **Monetizing Content and Microtransactions**: One of the primary benefits of integrating XRP into social media is its ability to support micropayments. Current payment systems often make it impractical to send or receive

small amounts of money due to high transaction fees and slow processing times. With XRP, social media platforms can introduce a seamless payment system where users can tip creators, pay for premium content, or unlock exclusive features with minimal friction.

For example, creators on platforms like YouTube, TikTok, or Instagram could receive instant payments for their content directly from their audience, without the need for intermediaries that typically take a substantial cut of earnings. This would democratize content monetization, allowing even smaller creators to earn directly from their followers without needing advertising revenue or brand sponsorships.

2. **Cross-Border Payments for Global Creators**: Many social media influencers and content creators operate on a global scale, often collaborating with brands and audiences from different countries. However, cross-border payments can be slow and expensive, especially when using traditional financial systems. XRP's ability to process international payments within seconds at a fraction of the cost can solve this problem, enabling creators to easily collect payments from fans, subscribers, and businesses anywhere in the world.

This would also simplify the payment process for businesses running global influencer campaigns or partnerships, making XRP an appealing solution for marketing on social media platforms.

Decentralizing Social Media with XRP and Blockchain

1. **Ownership of Content and Data**: One of the growing concerns with centralized social media platforms is the lack of control users have over their data and content. Currently, platforms like Facebook, Twitter, and Instagram hold immense control over user data, leading to issues like censorship, privacy violations, and monetization restrictions. By integrating blockchain technology, XRP can facilitate decentralized social media platforms where users have full control over their content, data, and earnings.

A blockchain-based social media platform powered by XRP could enable users to store and share content without relying on a central authority. Users could tokenize their posts, videos, or images, proving ownership and allowing them to directly sell or license their content. This shift toward decentralization would empower creators, reduce censorship, and create a more equitable digital landscape.

2. **Smart Contracts for Transparent Social Media Interactions**: XRP's blockchain can support smart contracts, which could automate and secure various aspects of social media interactions. For instance, smart contracts could be

used to set up automatic payments to content creators once certain engagement metrics are met (such as reaching a specific number of views or likes). This would reduce disputes over payouts, enhance transparency, and ensure that content creators are fairly compensated for their work.

Additionally, decentralized governance powered by XRP could allow users to vote on platform rules, content moderation, and other community decisions. This could lead to more democratic social media platforms where the community has greater input into how the platform operates.

Integrating XRP into Social Commerce

1. **Enabling Instant Purchases**: Social media platforms are increasingly merging with e-commerce, allowing users to buy products directly through posts or ads. XRP can streamline this process by enabling fast, direct payments between buyers and sellers. With XRP integrated into social media platforms, users could instantly purchase goods or services without needing to leave the app or rely on external payment gateways that add complexity to the transaction.

For businesses, especially smaller merchants and creators, XRP can reduce payment processing fees and ensure quicker settlement times. This would be particularly beneficial for global commerce, where businesses often face delays and high costs when dealing with cross-border transactions.

2. **Tokenizing Social Media Engagement**: Another potential use of XRP in social media is through tokenizing engagement. For example, users could earn tokens for interacting with posts, sharing content, or contributing to discussions, which could then be redeemed for services, products, or digital assets within the platform. This could create an ecosystem where user activity is directly tied to rewards, increasing engagement while providing real value.

Social platforms like Reddit have already experimented with tokens for community engagement, and XRP could take this concept to the next level by providing a more scalable and liquid form of digital currency that users can easily convert or use across different platforms.

Challenges and Considerations

Despite its potential, integrating XRP into social media comes with challenges. Regulatory uncertainty, especially in light of the ongoing legal case between Ripple and the U.S. Securities and Exchange Commission (SEC), could impact how easily XRP can be adopted by major platforms. Additionally, large social media companies may be slow to embrace decentralized models that reduce their control over user data and monetization systems.

Another challenge is user adoption. While XRP offers significant advantages, mainstream users may need time to become familiar with using cryptocurrency for transactions on social platforms. Ensuring a smooth and user-friendly experience will be crucial to driving widespread adoption.

XRP and the Future of Social Media: Unlocking Seamless Payments and Decentralized Content Platforms

XRP has the potential to revolutionize social media by creating faster, more affordable, and more inclusive payment systems. Whether through enabling seamless microtransactions, supporting decentralized platforms, or powering new forms of social commerce, XRP could reshape how creators monetize content and how users engage with platforms. However, the success of XRP in social media will depend on overcoming regulatory challenges, user adoption, and the willingness of platforms to embrace decentralized models. If these hurdles can be navigated, XRP could become a cornerstone of the social media landscape, fostering a new era of digital interactions.

X 21

21-XRP and the Future of Healthcare

As the healthcare industry undergoes digital transformation, the integration of blockchain technology and digital currencies like XRP is set to revolutionize how payments are processed, patient data is managed, and operational efficiency is enhanced. XRP, known for its speed, scalability, and low transaction costs, has the potential to address several key challenges in the healthcare sector, such as reducing administrative costs, improving cross-border payments, and ensuring data security through blockchain technology.

XRP's Role in Healthcare Payments

1. **Streamlining Payment Systems**: One of the most significant challenges in healthcare is the complex, multi-layered payment system. Medical billing and payments often involve insurance companies, patients, providers, and third-party processors, which can delay settlements and inflate

administrative costs. XRP's ability to settle payments in seconds at minimal cost can simplify this process. By enabling real-time payments between patients, providers, and insurers, XRP can help reduce delays, cut down on processing fees, and provide quicker reimbursement.

In particular, XRP's integration into healthcare payments could benefit medical tourism, where patients travel across borders to receive treatment. Cross-border transactions often come with high fees and long wait times, but XRP's decentralized system can facilitate instant, low-cost payments across countries. This would make it easier for patients and international healthcare providers to settle payments efficiently.

2. **Reducing Administrative Costs**: The healthcare industry is burdened with high administrative costs, much of which is tied to payment processing, billing errors, and claim disputes. XRP's blockchain technology can reduce these inefficiencies by providing transparency and automation in payment processing. Smart contracts powered by XRP could automate claims processing and ensure that payments are made once conditions, such as proof of service, are met. This would minimize disputes between insurers and providers and improve the overall efficiency of healthcare payments.

Data Security and Patient Privacy with XRP Blockchain

1. **Securing Patient Data**: Healthcare providers handle vast amounts of sensitive patient data, making data breaches a major concern. XRP's blockchain technology offers a decentralized, secure way to store and share health records while ensuring privacy. The decentralized nature of blockchain ensures that no single entity has control over patient data, and each transaction is recorded and encrypted, making it tamper-proof.

Using blockchain, healthcare providers can give patients more control over their health records, enabling them to share their data with trusted parties—such as doctors or specialists—without worrying about unauthorized access. This could lead to a more patient-centric approach, where individuals have greater control and transparency over how their data is used and who has access to it.

2. **Interoperability and Data Sharing**: One of the biggest challenges in healthcare is the lack of interoperability between different healthcare systems and institutions. XRP's blockchain could create a universal, secure platform for sharing patient data across hospitals, labs, pharmacies, and insurance providers. This would allow for seamless data exchange, improving the quality of care while reducing redundant tests and administrative bottlenecks.

Blockchain-based data sharing also ensures that patients' data is only accessible to authorized individuals or organizations, which could dramatically reduce issues related to data privacy and compliance with regulations like HIPAA (Health Insurance Portability and Accountability Act).

Enhancing Efficiency Through Blockchain and XRP

1. **Supply Chain Management**: In healthcare, managing the supply chain of pharmaceuticals, medical devices, and vaccines is a critical operation. XRP's blockchain can enhance supply chain transparency by enabling real-time tracking of products from manufacturer to patient. Every step of the supply chain can be recorded on the blockchain, ensuring that products are authentic and haven't been tampered with.

This system can help combat counterfeit drugs, ensure that medical supplies are properly stored and transported, and streamline logistics for hospitals and healthcare facilities. For instance, vaccines that require cold-chain logistics can be tracked through every stage of transport, ensuring compliance with temperature requirements and improving overall patient safety.

2. **Smart Contracts for Medical Agreements**: XRP's blockchain can support smart contracts, which

automate and enforce agreements once certain conditions are met. In healthcare, smart contracts could be used for a variety of purposes, such as ensuring that a medical device manufacturer is paid upon the delivery and confirmation of functional equipment, or automatically processing insurance claims based on the services provided.

Smart contracts can eliminate the need for intermediaries and reduce the time and resources spent on manual verification of contracts, allowing healthcare organizations to focus more on patient care and less on administrative tasks.

Cross-Border Health Services and Telemedicine

1. **Facilitating Payments for Telemedicine**: With the rapid growth of telemedicine, particularly during the COVID-19 pandemic, XRP's ability to provide instant cross-border payments could enable healthcare providers to easily offer services to international patients. XRP can simplify the payment process for remote consultations, making it easier for doctors to receive payments from patients in different countries without dealing with expensive transaction fees or currency conversion issues.
2. **Medical Tourism**: XRP also holds potential in the growing field of medical tourism. Patients seeking healthcare services abroad often face challenges related to payments, such as high currency conversion fees and slow international transfers. XRP can eliminate these issues by enabling

real-time, low-cost transactions that make it easier for international patients to pay for healthcare services in foreign countries.

Challenges and Considerations

While XRP offers significant advantages to the healthcare sector, challenges remain. The healthcare industry is highly regulated, and the adoption of new technologies, especially blockchain, may face resistance from institutions concerned with compliance, security, and privacy issues. Furthermore, the ongoing legal battle between Ripple and the U.S. Securities and Exchange Commission (SEC) over XRP's status as a security could impact the currency's future role in healthcare.

Additionally, the implementation of blockchain solutions in healthcare will require significant investment in infrastructure, as well as education and training for healthcare professionals to fully leverage the benefits of XRP and blockchain technology.

XRP and the Future of Healthcare: Transforming Payments, Data Security, and Efficiency

XRP has the potential to revolutionize the healthcare industry by providing faster, more affordable payment solutions, enhancing data security, and improving overall operational efficiency. Through its blockchain technology, XRP can address some of the key challenges facing the healthcare sector, from reducing administrative costs to ensuring the secure exchange of patient data. While hurdles related to regulation and adoption exist, XRP's integration into healthcare could lead to a more transparent, efficient, and patient-centric future for the industry.

X 22

22-XRP and the Future of Real Estate

The real estate industry, long known for its slow processes, high transaction costs, and reliance on intermediaries, is ripe for disruption by blockchain technology and digital currencies like XRP. As a fast, scalable, and cost-effective cryptocurrency, XRP has the potential to revolutionize the way property transactions are conducted, improve transparency, reduce costs, and introduce new efficiencies in property management. With blockchain at its core, XRP could reshape real estate markets by enabling smart contracts, facilitating cross-border transactions, and improving liquidity in a traditionally illiquid market.

XRP's Role in Real Estate Transactions

1. **Streamlining Property Sales and Transfers**: One of the most significant pain points in real estate transactions is the time and complexity involved in transferring property ownership. Traditional real estate deals require a range of intermediaries, including real estate agents,

title companies, and lawyers, which leads to high transaction costs and delays. XRP can facilitate faster, more direct payments between buyers and sellers, reducing reliance on third parties. The ability to settle payments in seconds, instead of days or weeks, could dramatically speed up the closing process, making real estate transactions more efficient.

2. **Lowering Transaction Costs**: Real estate transactions typically involve significant fees, such as closing costs, agent commissions, and transfer taxes. By using XRP for transactions, buyers and sellers could avoid many of these costs. The low transaction fees associated with XRP, coupled with the reduction in intermediary services, could save participants thousands of dollars per transaction. This would particularly benefit cross-border buyers who face additional costs related to currency conversion and international wire transfers.

3. **Enabling Global Real Estate Purchases**: The real estate market is increasingly global, with buyers from around the world investing in properties outside their home countries. However, cross-border real estate transactions are often complicated by currency exchange rates, international banking fees, and slow processing times. XRP's ability to process cross-border payments instantly at low cost makes it an ideal solution for global real estate purchases. Investors could easily purchase property anywhere in the world,

without worrying about the friction typically involved in international transactions.

Blockchain and Smart Contracts in Real Estate

1. **Smart Contracts for Secure and Automated Deals**: XRP's underlying blockchain technology can support smart contracts—self-executing contracts with the terms of the agreement directly written into code. In real estate, smart contracts can automate many aspects of the buying and selling process, ensuring that all conditions (such as inspections, financing approval, or title clearance) are met before the transaction is finalized.

For example, a smart contract could automatically transfer ownership of a property to the buyer and release funds to the seller once all parties have met the contract's conditions. This would eliminate the need for intermediaries like escrow agents, reduce the risk of fraud, and provide greater transparency in property transactions.

2. **Tokenization of Real Estate**: Blockchain enables the tokenization of real estate assets, which allows property owners to divide real estate into digital tokens that can be sold to multiple investors. This could transform the way people invest in real estate, making it easier for individuals to buy and sell fractional ownership of properties. XRP can facilitate the

purchase and transfer of these tokens, providing liquidity in an asset class that has traditionally been difficult to trade.

Tokenization also opens the door for smaller investors to access high-value properties that would otherwise be out of reach, democratizing real estate investment. With XRP, investors could easily trade their ownership stakes in real estate properties in a decentralized marketplace, similar to how stocks are traded on exchanges.

XRP and Real Estate Crowdfunding

1. **Expanding Access to Real Estate Investments**: XRP can play a crucial role in real estate crowdfunding platforms, where multiple investors pool funds to invest in a property. By using XRP, these platforms could offer a more transparent and efficient payment system, allowing investors from anywhere in the world to contribute to real estate projects in real-time, without the high fees and delays associated with traditional payment methods.

Real estate crowdfunding is particularly appealing for small investors who want to diversify their portfolios but lack the capital to purchase entire properties. XRP's fast and cost-effective transaction capabilities could enhance these platforms by making it easier for investors to participate, even with small amounts of capital.

2. **Improving Liquidity in Crowdfunding**: One of the challenges in real estate crowdfunding is liquidity—investors often have to wait months or years before they can sell their shares. With XRP and blockchain-based platforms, investors could trade their shares more easily on secondary markets, providing liquidity in what is traditionally a long-term and illiquid investment. This flexibility could attract more investors to real estate crowdfunding, further expanding access to real estate investments.

Property Management and XRP

1. **Efficient Rent Payments and Management**: XRP can streamline property management by enabling tenants to pay rent instantly and landlords to receive payments without the delays and fees associated with traditional banking systems. Using XRP, rent payments could be automated through smart contracts, ensuring that payments are made on time and recorded on the blockchain for full transparency.
2. **Maintenance and Repair Contracts**: Property management often involves contracts for services such as maintenance, repairs, and landscaping. Smart contracts powered by XRP could automate payments for these services, ensuring that vendors are paid immediately upon completion of their work. This would reduce administrative overhead for property managers and improve the efficiency of property upkeep.

Challenges and Considerations

Despite its potential, the adoption of XRP and blockchain technology in real estate faces several challenges. Regulatory uncertainty, particularly in the U.S., could slow down the adoption of XRP for real estate transactions. The ongoing legal battle between Ripple and the U.S. Securities and Exchange Commission (SEC) over whether XRP is classified as a security could impact its broader use in the real estate market.

Additionally, integrating blockchain technology into the real estate sector will require significant infrastructure development and a shift in how real estate professionals, buyers, and sellers operate. Educating stakeholders about the benefits of XRP and blockchain, as well as addressing security and privacy concerns, will be crucial to gaining widespread adoption.

XRP and the Future of Real Estate: Revolutionizing Transactions and Property Management

XRP's transformative potential in the real estate sector is not limited to specific regions but has a global impact, particularly in major real estate markets like the U.S., Japan, China, the UK, Europe, and the **BRICS** nations (Brazil, Russia, India, China, and South Africa). Across these regions,

XRP can modernize property transactions by making them faster, more cost-effective, and transparent.

In the **U.S.**, where real estate is heavily regulated and transactions involve multiple intermediaries, XRP could streamline the closing process by reducing reliance on costly third parties. Real estate deals in major U.S. markets such as New York, Los Angeles, and Miami would benefit from XRP's near-instant payment capabilities, especially for cross-border investors, who could avoid the lengthy settlement times and high fees currently associated with international transactions. Additionally, smart contracts powered by XRP could automate many elements of property transfers, reducing paperwork and increasing efficiency.

In **Japan**, where foreign investors, particularly from Asia and the West, have been steadily increasing their presence in the property market, XRP could enable seamless cross-border payments with minimal fees and delays. Japan's real estate market is seen as a stable investment hub, and XRP's integration could further enhance its attractiveness by removing barriers that traditionally slow down international property purchases.

China presents a unique opportunity for XRP. With capital controls and stringent regulations on foreign investments, XRP's decentralized, fast payment system could simplify cross-border property transactions for Chinese investors purchasing real estate abroad, as well as international buyers seeking opportunities within China. Its ability to bypass conventional banking processes could help navigate China's restrictions on capital outflow while complying with regulatory requirements.

In the **UK**, where real estate remains a preferred asset for global investors, particularly in London, XRP can play a critical role in increasing transaction efficiency. The UK's real estate market is heavily reliant on international buyers, and XRP could facilitate quicker, more secure cross-border deals. Blockchain-based property transfers could also appeal to international investors looking for more transparent and secure processes.

In **Europe**, where real estate markets like **Germany**, **France**, and **Spain** are prominent, XRP can provide greater liquidity to property investments and simplify cross-border transactions within the European Union (EU). The EU's commitment to embracing digital innovation means XRP's integration could further accelerate the digital transformation of property markets, making real estate investment more efficient and reducing bureaucratic obstacles.

When examining the **BRICS** nations—**Brazil**, **Russia**, **India**, **China**, and **South Africa**—the potential for XRP to revolutionize real estate transactions is substantial. These countries, with their rapidly growing real estate sectors, face challenges such as currency volatility, bureaucratic inefficiencies, and underdeveloped payment infrastructure. XRP can provide a solution by offering a stable, decentralized payment system that transcends borders and currencies.

- **Brazil**, with its booming real estate market, particularly in urban centers like São Paulo and Rio de Janeiro, could benefit from XRP's ability to offer fast, low-cost international payments, attracting more foreign investors to the country's growing housing and commercial real estate sectors.
- **Russia**, despite sanctions and financial constraints, could see XRP as a way to facilitate international real estate investments, enabling faster, more secure transactions for Russian investors looking to buy property abroad or attract foreign capital.
- **India**, one of the world's fastest-growing economies, has a rapidly expanding real estate market. XRP's blockchain technology could help modernize India's property transaction processes, making it easier for foreign investors to navigate India's real estate market while reducing administrative costs and delays.
- **South Africa**, which serves as a gateway for real estate investments in Africa, could leverage XRP to enable smoother cross-border transactions, attracting more international investors to its property market, especially in commercial and tourism-related real estate.

As XRP continues to gain traction, its role in the real estate markets of these major global regions, including the BRICS nations, could revolutionize how property is bought, sold, and managed. The cryptocurrency's ability to facilitate fast, cost-effective, and transparent transactions could democratize access to real estate investments, particularly in emerging markets, while making property ownership more accessible and efficient in developed economies. However, achieving this potential will depend on overcoming regulatory hurdles, ensuring broad adoption, and building the necessary blockchain infrastructure to support XRP's integration into the real estate sector. If these challenges are addressed, XRP could become a cornerstone in the future of global real estate, transforming how property transactions are conducted worldwide.

X 23

23-XRP and the Future of Energy

The energy sector, like many traditional industries, is experiencing rapid transformation as digital technologies and cryptocurrencies make inroads into operations, payments, and management. XRP, Ripple's digital currency known for its speed, scalability, and low-cost transactions, has the potential to revolutionize the energy market by streamlining payments, supporting decentralized energy systems, and fostering sustainability. As energy systems become more decentralized and integrated with blockchain technology, XRP can play a critical role in driving efficiency, transparency, and innovation in the future of energy.

XRP's Role in the Energy Market

1. **Efficient Payments in Energy Transactions**: One of the biggest challenges in the energy market is the complexity of payments, particularly for cross-border energy trading. The traditional system often involves intermediaries, delays, and high transaction costs, especially when it comes to international energy sales. XRP's fast, low-cost, and borderless

payment system can simplify these transactions, enabling instant settlements between energy producers, distributors, and consumers.

For example, energy companies operating in different countries could use XRP to settle payments in real-time, eliminating the need for currency conversion and reducing the time it takes to finalize deals. This would improve cash flow for energy companies and reduce the friction involved in global energy trade.

2. **Smart Grids and Decentralized Energy Systems**: As the world transitions to more decentralized energy systems, such as microgrids and peer-to-peer energy trading, XRP's blockchain technology can support the efficient transfer of value and energy across these networks. Decentralized energy markets allow consumers to buy and sell energy directly from one another, bypassing traditional utilities and creating more flexible, resilient systems.

XRP can enable seamless microtransactions in these decentralized energy markets, allowing consumers to pay for the exact amount of energy they use or sell surplus energy to others in real-time. This could be particularly impactful in regions where renewable energy sources, such as solar and wind, are becoming more common, as these sources often produce variable amounts of energy that need to be traded efficiently.

3. **Cross-Border Energy Payments**: Energy is a global commodity, with countries often relying on imports to meet their energy needs. Cross-border energy payments are traditionally slow and costly due to the involvement of banks, currency conversion, and settlement systems. XRP's ability to process cross-border payments in seconds at a fraction of the cost can transform how energy companies settle international transactions.

For instance, major energy exporters, such as oil and gas producers, could use XRP to streamline payments with international buyers, reducing delays and currency risks. This would be particularly beneficial for large-scale energy deals between countries, as it would reduce the cost and time associated with international wire transfers.

Blockchain and Energy Efficiency

1. **Optimizing Energy Supply Chains**: XRP's blockchain technology can enhance the transparency and efficiency of energy supply chains. By recording every transaction and transfer of energy on a distributed ledger, energy companies can track the origin, movement, and delivery of energy in real-time. This could reduce

inefficiencies, improve accountability, and help combat issues like energy theft or mismanagement.

Additionally, by integrating smart contracts into the energy supply chain, energy companies can automate payments and agreements once certain conditions are met. For example, a smart contract could automatically release payment once energy has been delivered and verified, reducing the need for intermediaries and improving cash flow for energy producers.

2. **Tokenizing Energy Assets**: Tokenization, the process of converting physical assets into digital tokens on a blockchain, could allow energy producers to tokenize energy assets such as solar panels, wind turbines, or even entire power plants. These tokens could then be traded or sold to investors, providing a new way for energy projects to raise capital. XRP could facilitate the purchase and transfer of these tokens, enabling more liquid and accessible energy markets.

This approach would open up energy investment to a wider range of participants, including small-scale investors who would otherwise be unable to invest in large energy projects. Tokenized energy assets could also be traded on secondary markets, providing liquidity in a traditionally illiquid asset class.

XRP's Role in Renewable Energy and Sustainability

1. **Promoting Clean Energy Adoption**: XRP's integration into energy markets could help promote the adoption of clean, renewable energy sources. Blockchain technology can provide greater transparency into the sourcing and use of renewable energy, allowing consumers and businesses to verify that the energy they purchase comes from sustainable sources. XRP could facilitate payments for renewable energy credits (RECs) or carbon offsets, ensuring that funds are efficiently transferred to support green energy initiatives.

Additionally, decentralized energy systems powered by XRP could make it easier for individuals and businesses to participate in renewable energy markets. For example, homeowners with solar panels could use XRP to sell excess energy to their neighbors, creating a more distributed and resilient energy grid.

2. **Energy Trading on Blockchain**: Energy trading between countries or corporations is often a slow and complex process, burdened by regulatory requirements and high costs. XRP's blockchain technology can simplify energy trading by allowing energy companies to trade directly with one another, reducing the need for intermediaries and speeding up settlement times. This would also enhance transparency, as all transactions would be recorded on a decentralized ledger, making it easier to verify the origin and volume of traded energy.

3. **Reducing the Environmental Impact of Crypto Mining**: While blockchain technology has the potential to improve the energy sector, concerns have been raised about the environmental impact of cryptocurrency mining, particularly for energy-intensive currencies like Bitcoin. XRP, however, is more energy-efficient compared to many other cryptocurrencies. Ripple's consensus mechanism, which does not rely on mining, consumes far less energy than proof-of-work systems like Bitcoin, making XRP a more sustainable choice for energy sector applications.

Challenges and Regulatory Considerations

While XRP's potential to transform the energy sector is significant, challenges remain, particularly around regulation. The energy market is heavily regulated, with different countries and regions implementing their own rules and standards for energy production, distribution, and trading. For XRP to be widely adopted, regulatory clarity on the use of digital currencies in energy transactions will be crucial. Additionally, ongoing legal challenges, such as Ripple's case with the U.S. Securities and Exchange Commission (SEC), could impact the pace of XRP's adoption in the energy market.

Furthermore, building the necessary blockchain infrastructure to support XRP's integration into the energy sector will require significant investment and collaboration between energy companies, regulators, and technology providers.

XRP and the Future of Energy: Powering Efficiency, Decentralization, and Sustainability

XRP holds the potential to significantly enhance the efficiency, decentralization, and sustainability of the global energy sector. By enabling near-instant, low-cost transactions, XRP can streamline the payment systems for energy markets, reducing the complexity and delays associated with traditional cross-border energy transactions. This increased efficiency is crucial for energy companies and consumers alike, as it simplifies international energy trading, accelerates settlements, and cuts down on administrative costs.

In terms of **decentralization**, XRP's integration with blockchain technology offers a foundation for the future of decentralized energy systems, such as microgrids and peer-to-peer energy trading. These systems empower individuals and communities to produce, sell, and buy energy directly, reducing reliance on centralized utilities. XRP's ability to facilitate microtransactions in real-time can ensure seamless energy exchanges in these decentralized networks, fostering more resilient and flexible energy ecosystems.

Sustainability is another key area where XRP can drive transformation. Its energy-efficient consensus mechanism makes it a greener alternative compared to other cryptocurrencies like Bitcoin, which have been criticized for their high energy consumption. Furthermore, XRP can support the growth of renewable energy markets by facilitating the transparent tracking and trading of renewable energy credits and carbon offsets. By providing a decentralized, transparent ledger for energy transactions, XRP can help ensure that funds flow efficiently to sustainable energy projects, accelerating the transition to a cleaner energy future.

In conclusion, XRP's unique capabilities make it an ideal tool for addressing the challenges of efficiency, decentralization, and sustainability in the energy sector. As the energy industry continues to evolve towards greener and more distributed systems, XRP is positioned to play a pivotal role in shaping the future of energy.

X 24

24-XRP *and the Future of Politics*

As cryptocurrencies and blockchain technologies become more integral to modern life, their potential impact on politics is increasingly apparent. XRP, Ripple's digital currency known for its fast and efficient cross-border transactions, offers unique capabilities that could transform political systems and financial interactions in the future. From decentralizing political donations to enhancing transparency and disrupting the global financial order, XRP is poised to play a significant role in shaping the political landscape of the 21st century.

XRP and Political Donations

1. **Decentralized Political Campaign Funding**: One of the most immediate and tangible ways XRP could influence politics is by decentralizing political donations. In many countries, political funding is tightly regulated, and campaign finance systems are often opaque and inefficient. With XRP, political donations can be made instantly,

transparently, and without the need for intermediaries like banks or payment processors.

Using XRP, political candidates or causes could receive contributions from supporters anywhere in the world with minimal transaction fees and real-time settlement. This could democratize political funding, giving smaller donors a more prominent role in the political process by reducing the transaction costs associated with traditional payment methods. Additionally, the transparency offered by XRP's blockchain technology could ensure that every contribution is traceable, reducing the risk of corruption and illegal donations that often plague campaign finance systems.

2. **Global Political Donations**: In an increasingly interconnected world, political movements are no longer confined to national borders. Movements like climate change activism or global human rights campaigns attract international supporters. XRP's ability to facilitate low-cost, cross-border transactions could enable global donors to contribute to political causes or candidates in other countries, bypassing the barriers of traditional financial systems. This could create a new form of international political engagement, where individuals from any part of the world can financially support political movements or causes they believe in.

XRP and Political Transparency

1. **Blockchain and Government Accountability**: Governments worldwide face ongoing challenges with transparency, particularly in how they manage public funds. XRP's blockchain technology offers a solution by creating an immutable ledger of transactions, ensuring that government spending and political donations are fully traceable. By using blockchain to record every transaction, politicians, government agencies, and campaign offices could be held accountable to their constituencies in real-time.

For instance, if governments adopt XRP's blockchain for budgeting, every dollar spent on public projects could be verified, reducing fraud and waste. This level of transparency could also be applied to international aid, where donor countries or organizations could track how their funds are used, ensuring that money is not diverted for corrupt purposes.

2. **Election Integrity and Smart Contracts**: The transparency of blockchain technology also opens the door to potential improvements in election integrity. Smart contracts powered by XRP could automate various aspects of the voting process, ensuring that elections are free from manipulation. For example, smart contracts could automatically count votes

or distribute election funds once pre-agreed conditions are met, minimizing human error or fraud in electoral processes.

Blockchain-based voting systems could also provide voters with more trust in election outcomes, as all transactions (i.e., votes) would be publicly visible on a decentralized ledger, making tampering nearly impossible. While integrating blockchain into electoral systems faces numerous challenges—such as security concerns and infrastructure development—it could be a major step toward enhancing the legitimacy of democratic systems around the world.

XRP and Global Financial Politics

1. **Disrupting the Global Financial Order**: XRP's ability to facilitate instant, low-cost cross-border transactions gives it the potential to disrupt the current global financial order, where established institutions like SWIFT and traditional banking systems dominate international payments. The speed and efficiency of XRP could make it a preferred currency for international trade and financial exchanges, reducing the reliance on traditional financial infrastructure.

This could have profound political implications. For instance, countries currently excluded from the global financial system due to sanctions or restrictions could adopt XRP to bypass international barriers. This would not only challenge the dominance of the U.S. dollar as the world's reserve currency but also undermine the political leverage that countries like the United States wield through economic sanctions. The decentralization of global financial systems, driven by XRP and other cryptocurrencies, could shift geopolitical power away from traditional financial centers toward more decentralized, tech-driven economies.

2. **Monetary Sovereignty and Central Bank Digital Currencies (CBDCs)**: Many governments are already exploring the development of Central Bank Digital Currencies (CBDCs) as a response to the rise of cryptocurrencies like XRP. As countries like China, the EU, and the U.S. explore the implementation of their own digital currencies, the political power associated with monetary sovereignty will come into sharper focus.

While CBDCs are state-backed, XRP represents a decentralized alternative that could challenge the power of central banks. XRP's ability to offer fast, transparent transactions without the need for state intervention means it could coexist with or even outcompete CBDCs in some cases, further decentralizing the global financial system. In such a scenario, governments would need to adapt their monetary policies and international trade strategies to account for the rising influence of decentralized currencies like XRP.

Challenges and Regulatory Hurdles

While XRP has the potential to significantly reshape the political landscape, it faces regulatory challenges that must be addressed. One of the primary hurdles is how governments classify and regulate cryptocurrencies. In many countries, there is still uncertainty about whether digital currencies like XRP should be treated as securities, commodities, or currencies. In the U.S., for example, the ongoing legal battle between Ripple and the Securities and Exchange Commission (SEC) regarding XRP's classification could set a precedent for how cryptocurrencies are regulated globally.

Additionally, governments may resist adopting decentralized currencies like XRP due to concerns about losing control over monetary policy and financial stability. The political power that comes from controlling a national currency could be eroded if decentralized currencies gain widespread adoption, leading to increased scrutiny and tighter regulation of XRP and similar technologies.

XRP and the Main Political Challenges Ahead

While XRP holds immense potential to reshape the political landscape by promoting decentralization, transparency, and efficiency, it also faces significant political challenges that could impact its adoption and influence. One of the most pressing issues is **regulatory uncertainty**. Governments and regulatory bodies, particularly in the U.S., are grappling with how to classify and regulate cryptocurrencies like XRP. The ongoing legal dispute between Ripple and the U.S. Securities and Exchange Commission (SEC) over whether XRP should be considered a security exemplifies this challenge. The outcome of this case will not only affect Ripple and XRP but could set a broader precedent for how cryptocurrencies are regulated globally.

Another major concern is **monetary sovereignty**. Governments may see the rise of decentralized currencies like XRP as a threat to their control over national currencies and monetary policy. If XRP and other cryptocurrencies gain widespread adoption, central banks could lose their ability to influence inflation, interest rates, and economic stability through traditional tools. This could lead to increased government resistance to the widespread adoption of decentralized financial systems and prompt stricter regulations on the use of digital currencies in political and financial systems.

Additionally, **geopolitical tensions** could emerge as decentralized currencies like XRP offer ways to bypass economic sanctions and financial controls. Countries under sanctions or financial restrictions may turn to XRP and other cryptocurrencies to circumvent traditional banking systems, potentially undermining the effectiveness of sanctions as a tool for international diplomacy. This could lead to increased scrutiny and regulation of XRP's use in international financial transactions, particularly by countries that rely on sanctions as part of their foreign policy.

Finally, **cybersecurity and election integrity** remain critical concerns. While blockchain technology promises transparency and security, implementing decentralized voting systems or political donations powered by XRP could face cyber threats. Governments must ensure that these systems are secure and resistant to hacking or manipulation before integrating them into their political processes.

In conclusion, while XRP offers significant opportunities for decentralizing and transforming political systems, it must overcome substantial political challenges. Regulatory clarity, government concerns over monetary sovereignty, the geopolitical implications of decentralized currencies, and cybersecurity issues will all play key roles in determining whether XRP can fulfill its potential in the political realm. Addressing these challenges will be crucial for XRP's future in politics, and its ability to create more transparent, efficient, and decentralized systems of governance and finance.

X 25

25-XRP and the Future of Philanthropy

As the world of philanthropy evolves alongside technological advancements, cryptocurrencies like XRP are poised to play a significant role in shaping the future of charitable giving. XRP, with its fast, secure, and low-cost transactions, offers new opportunities for nonprofits, donors, and recipients to engage in philanthropy more efficiently and transparently. From streamlining cross-border donations to enhancing transparency and accountability, XRP's blockchain technology can transform how charitable organizations operate and maximize their global impact.

XRP and Efficient Donations

1. **Low-Cost, Instant Donations**: One of the most significant barriers to effective philanthropy is the high transaction costs associated with traditional payment systems. When donors contribute to charities, a portion of the donation is often lost to fees from banks, credit card

companies, or payment processors. XRP's low transaction fees and ability to process payments in seconds make it an ideal solution for charitable organizations looking to maximize the value of every donation.

By accepting XRP, nonprofits can reduce the friction of receiving donations, ensuring that more funds reach those in need. This efficiency is especially beneficial for international charities, where cross-border donations typically come with currency conversion fees and long processing times. XRP's decentralized nature allows donations to be sent globally without the delays or high costs traditionally associated with international transfers.

2. **Micropayments and Crowdfunding**: XRP's efficiency also enables the use of micropayments, which opens up new possibilities for philanthropy. Many individuals may not feel comfortable making large donations but would be willing to contribute small amounts. XRP's low transaction fees make it feasible to collect and process these smaller donations, which can accumulate to make a substantial impact.

For instance, crowdfunding campaigns could leverage XRP to allow global donors to contribute small amounts toward causes they care about, without worrying about losing a significant portion of their donation to processing fees. This could democratize philanthropy, making it easier for people from all walks of life to participate in charitable giving.

Transparency and Accountability in Philanthropy

1. **Blockchain for Transparent Donations**: A key challenge in philanthropy is ensuring that donations are used effectively and ethically. Donors often want to know how their contributions are being spent, but traditional financial systems offer limited transparency. XRP's blockchain technology offers a solution by providing a decentralized, transparent ledger of transactions. Every donation made via XRP can be traced on the blockchain, allowing donors to see exactly where their money is going.

This level of transparency can build greater trust between donors and charitable organizations, as it ensures that funds are being allocated as promised. Charities that adopt XRP's blockchain for financial management can offer real-time updates on how donations are being spent, whether it's on operational costs, projects, or directly to beneficiaries.

2. **Smart Contracts for Conditional Giving**: XRP's blockchain also supports smart contracts, which can be used to automate and enforce conditions on charitable donations. For example, a donor could specify that their donation only be released when certain milestones are met, such as the completion of a building project or the

distribution of resources to a specified number of beneficiaries.

Smart contracts could ensure that donations are used effectively by triggering payments only when the predefined conditions are met. This would reduce the risk of mismanagement or fraud, giving donors more control over how their contributions are used.

Global Philanthropy and Cross-Border Giving

1. **Enabling Cross-Border Donations**: XRP's ability to facilitate instant, low-cost cross-border payments can significantly enhance the reach of global philanthropy. Donors can contribute to causes and organizations anywhere in the world, without the delays and fees associated with traditional banking systems. This is particularly important for charities operating in developing countries, where financial infrastructure may be limited and international transfers are slow and expensive.

With XRP, international donors can send funds directly to charitable organizations in regions where they are needed most, ensuring that donations arrive quickly and efficiently. This could be particularly impactful in response to global crises, such as natural disasters or humanitarian emergencies, where immediate financial support is essential.

2. **Reaching Underbanked Communities**: Many communities in need of charitable assistance are located in regions where access to traditional banking is limited. XRP's decentralized, blockchain-based system allows charitable organizations to reach these underbanked populations more effectively. By enabling direct, peer-to-peer donations through XRP, nonprofits can bypass the need for traditional banking systems and get funds directly to those who need them.

This decentralized approach also reduces the need for intermediaries, such as banks or third-party financial institutions, which often take a portion of the donation as a fee. By removing these intermediaries, XRP ensures that more of the donation goes directly to the cause, increasing the overall impact of philanthropic efforts.

Innovative Uses of XRP in Philanthropy

1. **Tokenizing Charitable Assets**: XRP's blockchain technology can also be used to tokenize charitable assets. For example, organizations could create digital tokens representing real-world assets, such as food, medical supplies, or educational materials. These tokens could then be distributed to beneficiaries, ensuring that donations are used to provide essential resources rather than being diverted for other purposes.

This system would create a transparent and efficient way to manage charitable resources, with donors able to see exactly how their contributions are being transformed into tangible support for those in need. Additionally, tokenization could open up new fundraising methods for charities, allowing them to offer unique digital assets in exchange for donations.

2. **Crypto-Backed Endowments**: Charities could also explore the use of crypto-backed endowments or funds. By holding XRP in a charitable endowment, organizations could benefit from the potential appreciation of digital assets over time. This would allow charities to increase their financial sustainability while providing a new revenue stream for their philanthropic efforts.

As cryptocurrencies become more widely adopted, holding XRP could become a strategic financial decision for nonprofits looking to diversify their funding sources and ensure long-term viability.

Challenges and Considerations

While XRP offers significant advantages to the future of philanthropy, challenges remain. One of the primary concerns is regulatory uncertainty. Cryptocurrencies, including XRP, face varying regulations across different jurisdictions, and charities may need to navigate complex legal frameworks to accept and manage digital assets. In some countries, cryptocurrencies are still viewed with skepticism or are heavily regulated, which could limit the adoption of XRP in the nonprofit sector.

Additionally, there is a need to educate donors and charitable organizations about the benefits and risks associated with cryptocurrencies. Many traditional donors may be unfamiliar with digital currencies, and charities may be hesitant to adopt them due to concerns about volatility, security, and legal compliance.

Transforming Donations, Transparency, and Global Impact with XRP

XRP stands at the forefront of transforming the future of philanthropy, offering innovative solutions that can radically enhance the way donations are made, tracked, and utilized for global impact. By enabling **low-cost, instant donations**, XRP can remove the barriers of traditional financial systems, ensuring that more funds reach charitable causes quickly and with minimal loss to transaction fees. This is particularly impactful in cross-border philanthropy, where XRP's speed and efficiency allow global donors to support causes anywhere in the world, extending the reach of charitable organizations and empowering international collaboration.

In terms of **transparency**, XRP's blockchain technology provides a level of accountability that is unmatched by traditional financial systems. Donors can track their contributions in real-time, seeing exactly where their money goes and how it is used, building greater trust between nonprofits and their supporters. This transparency also benefits the nonprofits, as they can demonstrate financial integrity and efficiency, ensuring that donations are being spent in ways that align with their mission and values.

The **global impact** of XRP on philanthropy cannot be overstated. By facilitating donations to underbanked communities and regions with limited access to traditional financial infrastructure, XRP opens new pathways for charities to operate in areas where they are needed most. Its ability to bypass traditional banking systems and intermediaries allows charities to maximize the effectiveness of every donation, ensuring that funds directly reach those in need, especially in times of crisis or humanitarian emergencies.

XRP's role in transforming donations, promoting transparency, and amplifying global impact makes it a powerful tool for the future of philanthropy. As more charitable organizations and donors embrace the potential of cryptocurrency, XRP could reshape the landscape of global giving, driving greater efficiency, trust, and accessibility in the world of philanthropy.

Jon Erlaitz

X 589

26-Why XRP Is the Future of Digital Currency

As the world continues to shift toward a more digital and interconnected economy, the need for fast, efficient, and scalable digital currencies has never been more apparent. Among the numerous cryptocurrencies in circulation, **XRP** stands out as one of the most promising digital currencies for the future. Created by Ripple Labs, XRP is designed to facilitate cross-border payments and address many of the inefficiencies that plague traditional financial systems. With its ability to process transactions quickly and at low cost, its scalability, and its potential for widespread global adoption, XRP is poised to become a cornerstone of the evolving digital currency landscape.

1. Speed and Efficiency in Cross-Border Payments

One of XRP's most significant advantages is its ability to facilitate near-instant cross-border payments. Traditional payment systems, such as SWIFT or bank wire transfers, often take days to process international transactions, incurring high fees along the way. XRP, by contrast, can process payments in a matter of seconds, regardless of the geographic locations involved. Its **transaction confirmation time of around 3-5 seconds** is a significant improvement over traditional financial systems and even other popular cryptocurrencies like Bitcoin or Ethereum, which can take much longer due to their reliance on energy-intensive mining processes.

This speed not only benefits consumers making international payments but also has the potential to transform industries such as remittances, global trade, and e-commerce, where fast, reliable payments are critical. By eliminating the delays and costs associated with traditional banking systems, XRP is well-suited for global financial transactions and stands as a more efficient alternative to legacy systems.

2. Low Transaction Costs

While many cryptocurrencies, especially Bitcoin, face criticism for their high transaction fees—particularly during times of network congestion—XRP boasts consistently low fees, typically a fraction of a cent per transaction. This makes it ideal for a wide range of use cases, from **microtransactions** to **high-value transfers**.

XRP's low transaction fees are particularly advantageous for industries that rely on small payments, such as content monetization, gaming, and micropayments. Whether it's paying for digital services or transferring money between users, XRP offers a more cost-effective solution compared to both traditional financial services and many other cryptocurrencies.

3. Scalability

As the global demand for digital payments continues to grow, scalability is a critical factor in determining the success of any digital currency. Many cryptocurrencies face scalability challenges, where increased usage leads to slower transactions and higher fees. XRP, however, is built to handle **1,500 transactions per second (TPS)**, significantly more than Bitcoin's average of 7 TPS and Ethereum's average of 15-30 TPS.

This scalability makes XRP one of the few digital currencies capable of meeting the needs of a global financial system. Whether used by large institutions or individual users, XRP can handle the volume of transactions required to support global commerce and finance, all without compromising speed or efficiency.

4. Strong Institutional Support and Use Cases

XRP's real-world utility is further strengthened by its **adoption by financial institutions**. Ripple, the company behind XRP, has formed partnerships with over 300 financial institutions, including major banks, payment providers, and remittance companies. These institutions use Ripple's technology, including XRP, to improve cross-border payments and streamline international money transfers.

XRP is integrated into RippleNet, a global payments network that allows banks and financial institutions to settle transactions in real-time. This network provides a compelling alternative to traditional correspondent banking and reduces reliance on pre-funded accounts (known as nostro accounts) by using XRP as a bridge currency. This real-world adoption is a critical differentiator for XRP, as it is not just a speculative asset but also serves a clear, functional purpose within the financial system.

5. Environmental Sustainability

Environmental concerns around cryptocurrency mining, particularly with proof-of-work systems like Bitcoin, have become a hot topic. The energy-intensive mining processes of many digital currencies have raised alarms about their sustainability and long-term viability. XRP, however, uses a **consensus algorithm** that does not rely on mining, making it much more energy-efficient.

Ripple has emphasized sustainability, and XRP's design reflects this commitment. With the increasing focus on reducing carbon footprints, XRP's environmentally friendly consensus mechanism offers a significant advantage for organizations looking to adopt digital currencies while minimizing their environmental impact.

6. Potential for Regulatory Clarity and Compliance

One of the biggest challenges for the cryptocurrency space is regulatory uncertainty, which can hinder the growth and adoption of digital currencies. XRP, despite facing its own regulatory challenges (most notably with the U.S. Securities and Exchange Commission), is designed to comply with the global financial system's regulatory frameworks. Ripple has actively worked with regulators around the world to create a compliant and secure platform for financial institutions to use XRP for cross-border payments.

As global regulatory clarity around digital currencies improves, XRP is well-positioned to benefit from its established relationships with financial institutions and regulators. This proactive approach to compliance increases confidence in XRP's future viability as a mainstream digital currency.

7. Global Adoption and Use Cases

XRP's global adoption is another factor that sets it apart from many other cryptocurrencies. Ripple's focus on international markets has helped XRP gain traction in regions where traditional banking infrastructure is either underdeveloped or inefficient. For example, XRP has been integrated into various remittance platforms, enabling fast, low-cost transfers to regions like **Southeast Asia, Africa, and Latin America**.

As more businesses, individuals, and financial institutions recognize the benefits of XRP, its use cases will continue to expand, further embedding the currency into global financial systems. This global footprint is crucial for XRP's longevity and positions it as a currency capable of facilitating transactions across borders and industries.

Speed, Efficiency, and Global Adoption

XRP's unique combination of speed, scalability, low transaction costs, environmental sustainability, and strong institutional support makes it a standout digital currency with the potential to transform the global financial system. As cross-border payments become increasingly important in a globalized economy, XRP offers a more efficient, cost-effective, and sustainable solution than many traditional systems or even other cryptocurrencies.

Moreover, XRP's ability to integrate with existing financial infrastructure and comply with regulatory requirements positions it for long-term success in the evolving digital currency space. As global adoption grows and more industries embrace digital currencies for payments, remittances, and commerce, XRP is well-positioned to become a cornerstone of the future financial landscape, driving innovation and efficiency in the digital economy.

In this New Edition I want to give you a new present:

The Global XRP-ETF Revolution, a guide to understand and check all the ETF based on XRP.

Global XRP-ETF Revolution

And much more ...

Special Gift

Thank you so much for purchasing Mastering XRP!

If you find value in the book, I would be incredibly grateful if you could take a moment to leave a review. Your feedback helps other readers discover the book and supports my journey as an author.

Scan this QR to download this ebook and increase your knowledge in the XRP World.

In this ebook you will improve your knowledge in the XRP world, discover the future of XRP and Financial Inclusion, your role as an investor and more resources for further exploration.

Enjoy your gift and I wish for everyone reading this book to become happy, rich and be in peace for lifetime.

Jon Erlaitz

www.ingramcontent.com/pod-product-compliance
Lightning Source LLC
LaVergne TN
LVHW100303210926
848480LV00003B/1011